WORLD WAR II VERTICAL ENVELOPMENT: THE GERMAN INFLUENCE ON
U.S. ARMY AIRBORNE OPERATIONS

A thesis presented to the Faculty of the U.S. Army
Command and General Staff College in partial
fulfillment of the requirements for the
degree

MASTER OF MILITARY ART AND SCIENCE
Military History

by

THOMAS J. SHEEHAN, MAJ, USA
B.S., United States Military Academy, 1991

Fort Leavenworth, Kansas
2003

Approved for public release; distribution is unlimited.

MASTER OF MILITARY ART AND SCIENCE

THESIS APPROVAL PAGE

Name of Candidate: Thomas J. Sheehan

Thesis Title: World War II Vertical Envelopment: The German Influence on U.S. Army Airborne Operations

Approved by:

_____, Thesis Committee Chairman
Bruce W. Menning, Ph.D.

_____, Member
LTC Paul L. Cal, M.A.

_____, Member
LTC John A. Suprin, M.A.

Accepted this 6th day of June 2003 by:

_____, Director, Graduate Degree Programs
Philip J. Brookes, Ph.D.

The opinions and conclusions expressed herein are those of the student author and do not necessarily represent the views of the U.S. Army Command and General Staff College or any other governmental agency. (References to this study should include the foregoing statement.)

ABSTRACT

WORLD WAR II VERTICAL ENVELOPMENT: THE GERMAN INFLUENCE ON U.S. ARMY AIRBORNE OPERATIONS, by MAJ Thomas J. Sheehan, 100 pages.

This study traces the development of the United States Army's airborne concept during World War II. More than any other precedent, German airborne operations against Crete influenced the evolution of U.S. Army airborne doctrine, organization and utilization. Consequently, this thesis adopts a comparative perspective, both direct and longitudinal to examine the U.S. and German airborne experiences, with an emphasis on the former.

A series of concerns and issues, including doctrine, organization, technology, tactics, and procedures, focus comparative emphasis on the U.S. airborne from 1940 through July 1943. The formative period extended through May 1941, while the expansion years extended into 1943. A major point of departure and comparison is the German invasion of Crete in May 1941, which lent important impetus to U.S. airborne development. Without knowledge of German losses and shortcoming, U.S. planners accepted Crete as their model on which to base rapid airborne expansion. Subsequently, Operation Husky, the invasion of Sicily, taught U.S. airborne planners how to evolve their own lessons learned in detail and in full context. Crete remained the inspiration, but not the roadmap.

ACKNOWLEDGMENTS

I would like to thank my wife, Robin D. Sheehan, a tremendous paratrooper, leader, and the first female Command Sergeant Major to ever serve in the 82nd Airborne Division. It was she who encouraged me to devote the time and energy necessary for this MMAS thesis. Second, I owe thanks to my thesis committee, Dr. Bruce Menning, LTC Paul Cal, and LTC John Suprin, for guiding me down the path and subsequently keeping me on azimuth. I could not have faced the challenge without their efforts. To all the paratroopers with whom I have served past and present, thank you for your efforts in protecting our country and for instilling a love in me for our profession. Finally, to all the veterans of this nation's past conflicts, thank you for leaving a tradition of honor and prestige, and for setting high standards for future generations of soldiers to aspire and to attain.

TABLE OF CONTENTS

	Page
THESIS APPROVAL PAGE	ii
ABSTRACT	iii
ACKNOWLEDGMENTS	iv
ACRONYMS	vi
ILLUSTRATIONS	vii
TABLES	viii

CHAPTER

1. INTRODUCTION	1
2. THE FORMATIVE YEARS: 1940-1941	13
3. THE INVASION OF CRETE	31
4. THE EXPANSION YEARS: 1941 – 1943	45
5. THE U.S. AIRBORNE IN ACTION – OPERATION HUSKY	57
6. CONCLUSION	74

APPENDIX

A. U.S. AND GERMAN RANK EQUIVALENTS	83
GLOSSARY	84
SOURCES CONSULTED	85
INITIAL DISTRIBUTION LIST	90
CERTIFICATION FOR MMAS DISTRIBUTION STATEMENT	91

ACRONYMS

AIR	Airborne Infantry Regiment. A glider equipped regiment within U.S. Army airborne units.
CG	Combat Glider. The two-letter designator, followed by a number (i.e.: CG-4) for American gliders utilized during World War II.
DFS	*Deutsches Forschungsinstitut für Segelflugzeug*. The three-letter designator, followed by a number (i.e.: DFS-230) for German gliders utilized during World War II.
DZ	Drop Zone. Area denoted on the ground where paratroopers or gliders are expected to land.
FM	Field Manual. A U.S. Army document that outlines approved doctrine, tactics, techniques, and procedures for units in both training and combat.
PIB	Parachute Infantry Battalion. A parachute equipped battalion within U.S. Army airborne units, normally comprised of three rifle companies and a headquarters company.
PIR	Parachute Infantry Regiment. A parachute equipped regiment within U.S. Army airborne units, normally comprised of nine rifle companies and three headquarters companies.
RCT	Regimental Combat Team. A combined arms organization within U.S. Army combat units normally comprised of an infantry regiment and associated combat support and service support units.
RZ	*Rückenfallschirm Zwangsauslösung*. The two-letter designator, followed by a number (i.e.: RZ-16) for German parachutes utilized during World War II.

ILLUSTRATIONS

Figure	Page
1. German Command Structure for Operation Mercury	33
2. Assault on Crete	35
3. 505th RCT Planned DZs	61
4. Actual Landings of 505th and 504th	67

TABLES

Table	Page
1. U.S. and German Airborne Capability Comparison (May 1941)	28
2. Number of C-47s Procured by Army Air Forces: Jan 1940-Dec 1945	50
3. Total Number of Gliders Procured By Army Air Forces, 1940-1945	53

CHAPTER 1

INTRODUCTION

This study traces the evolution of United States Army airborne forces and doctrine from the original test platoon in July 1940 to the invasion of Sicily in July 1943. The seeds were planted at Fort Benning, Georgia with 55 pioneers and bore fruit three short years later with five Airborne Divisions and numerous separate battalions and regiments. Shaping this evolution were many men and many influences, including vicarious combat experience.

This thesis focuses on the role that the German airborne operation during the invasion of Crete, 20-31 May 1941, played in the development of United States airborne doctrine and employments during World War II. It is a study of German airborne doctrine and airborne organization for the invasion of Crete. It is also a comparative study that focuses on American airborne doctrine, force and command structures, tactics, techniques, and procedures before and after the invasion of Crete. The object of comparison is to determine whether the United States airborne doctrine introduced its own model, adopted the German model, or evolved as a hybrid of the two. Analysis of the first major U.S. application of airborne warfare in the European Theater of Operations, Operation Husky, (the invasion of Sicily), tests the comparative proposition.

The airborne operations conducted in Sicily and Crete were as similar as they were different. Both were sideshows conducted against islands in the Mediterranean that figured only peripherally in the major strategic objectives of their respective planners. Hitler was preoccupied with the coming invasion of Russia, and the United States preferred a cross-Channel invasion of the European continent. Crete fell almost entirely to paratroop, glider, and airlanding forces; Sicily fell to a combined airborne and amphibious operation. Both invasions were ultimately successful, but neither was without major flaws. Whereas Crete became the graveyard for German airborne operations, the United States moved on after Sicily to employ its airborne forces with a great degree of success in both the European and Pacific Theaters of Operations.

U.S. airborne development is a significant research topic for at least three primary reasons. First, it addresses an area in which little research has been done. Several sources evaluate German operations in Crete, while numerous other sources detail the rapid expansion of American airborne forces in 1942. However, very few analyses draw comparisons between the two. A second reason for studying this topic relates to force projection. In today's military, force projection is imperative, since the Army has moved to a predominately CONUS-based force. Many of the lessons learned from the 1940's retain relevance today. Current U.S. airborne forces comprise a rapid-deployment, strategic force. However, the success of their employment turns on many of the lessons learned during World War II application. A 1947-quote from James Gavin applies as much today as it did then:

> The knowledge of the existence of a well trained airborne army, capable of moving anywhere on the globe on short notice, available to an international security body such as the United Nations, is our best guarantee of lasting peace. And the nation or nations that control the air will control the peace.[1]

A third reason for an examination of U.S. airborne development relates to contemporary preoccupations with the Objective Force. The original 1999 Objective Force White Papers called for each Unit of Action within the Objective Force to have a forced entry requirement, necessitating vertical envelopment capabilities at the tactical level of warfare.[2] The most recent version of the White Papers identifies Special Purpose units consisting of Airborne, Air Assault, and Special Operations Forces as augmentees to Units of Employment.[3] Regardless of the requirement, the forcible entry capability remains important as the Army continues the Transformation process. Emphasis on this capability represents a significant change in current force structure and capabilities across the entire U.S. Army spectrum. Many of the lessons learned with regard to theories, training, doctrine, and applications from the "birth" of the U.S. Army's airborne capabilities retain relevance for development of the Objective Force. Currently, the Objective Force is entirely doctrine based. Changes in organization, equipment, and force structure go hand-in-hand with developments in science and technology. During the early 1940s, the same was true for U.S. airborne forces. Analysis of that experience promises to add depth and insight to current organizational and doctrinal endeavors.

Throughout military history, commanders have attempted to develop different ways and means with which to envelop their enemy on the field of battle. Until the advent of airborne and glider forces, terrain and enemy defensive arrays restricted the attacker's options to frontal assault or envelopment. Generations of military leaders have wrestled with the validity of Clausewitz's assessment of the complexities of two-dimensional warfare.

Since the beginning of time, man has attempted to gain offensive advantage over his opponent on the field of battle. The Greeks developed the phalanx, Alexander the Great mastered the use of cavalry, the Romans created road networks to rapidly move their Legions, Frederick the Great developed the Oblique Order, and Napoleon overwhelmed his enemies through his use of strategic and tactical maneuver. Throughout history, men sought to convert technological advances into greater mobility and striking power for their armed forces.

Many inventions have been born out of a specific, often urgent need for their use. The parachute, however, was not one of them. The possibility of adding a third dimension to ground warfare, with all of its promise, was recognized long before technology caught up with the tactical dream.

For centuries, strategists had envisioned the capabilities presented by an airborne force. In the fifteenth century, Leonardo da Vinci described what is believed to be the first practical model of a parachute in his *Codex Atlanticus* manuscript, "If a man have a tent of linen of which the apertures have all been stopped up...he will be able to throw himself down from any great height without sustaining any injury."[4]

In November 1783, Francois Pilatre de Rozier and the Marquis d'Arlandes became the first men to ascend in free flight with a hot-air balloon. Two weeks later, two other Frenchmen, Jacques Charles and Aine Robert, used a hydrogen balloon for a longer flight, their achievement cheered on by a delirious crowd of nearly 500,000 onlookers. Amidst of the excitement of these early flights, their military significance passed almost unnoticed. One spectator, the American scholar, scientist, and statesman, Benjamin Franklin, wrote in January of 1784:

> And where is the Prince who can so afford to cover his country with troops for its defense, as that ten thousand men descending from the clouds might not in many places do an infinite deal of mischief before a force could be brought together to repel them?[5]

It would be a century and a half before this dream would become a practicable. In the meantime, men and women alike began to entertain crowds with death-defying leaps from balloons with parachutes. Throughout the 1800s, daredevils made numerous jumps, thrilling circus audiences across the world. With the exception of jumps from balloons at increasingly higher altitudes, parachuting and parachute development evolved slowly. The invention of the airplane and the subsequent high death rate resulting from crashes caused the next series of improvements in parachute design.

The United States began its preliminary ascent into the military world of parachutes during World War I. Colonel William "Billy" Mitchell is credited with originating the vertical envelopment maneuver. He was initially infatuated with German aviators being able to parachute from their stricken planes, a luxury the Allied pilots did not have, and he attempted to rectify the problem. He initiated experimental studies in the fall of 1918 to develop parachutes for his aviators.[6] He also approached General John "Black Jack" Pershing with a plan to parachute infantrymen behind German lines and link them up with a coordinated ground attack. Mitchell's plan was startling in its originality. He envisioned the delivery of 12,000 men from the 1st Infantry Division, the pride of the American Expeditionary Force. The proposal relied heavily upon large numbers of parachutes and aircraft, neither of which were available in sufficient quantities. Further, the size, depth, and distance of the operation would place impossible demands on U.S. Army communications, logistics, and command and control.[7] Pershing rejected the idea just as the armistice ended the war. Mitchell had seen the same vision as fellow countryman Benjamin Franklin. The technology necessary to make it work was still not fully available. Additionally, the military world was not mentally prepared for the idea of airborne warfare. The "war to end all wars" temporarily ended the idea of parachuting soldiers into enemy territory on a grand scale.

During 1918-1939, two prevailing schools of thought pondered the nature of future war. Many believed it would be an extension of the trench warfare that characterized World War I, still called The Great War. The static positions of the French Maginot Line clearly reflected this belief on a national level. Many others believed that maneuver warfare focused on armored thrusts would dominate, as the Germans would demonstrate with their violent and effective Blitzkrieg tactics.[8] The shape of warfare was changing dramatically as nations prepared to fight again on a global scale. World War II demanded tactical innovation to prevent repetition of the static trench warfare of World War I and to overcome the technological and tactical advances made since 1918. One innovation was airborne warfare.

The years following the 1918 armistice brought worldwide revulsion against the horrors of war and a waning of intellectual vigor in military circles. In the United States, World War I was viewed as an aberration. Participation in the war provided no real test of American strategic doctrine and, after the armistice, in typical American reaction to war, the nation rushed to redeploy its soldiers, demobilize, and forget the aberration.

During the interwar years, a popular belief that the United States should neither enter into military alliances, nor maintain military forces capable of offensive action, deeply influenced national policy. Under these conditions, and in the interest of the national economy, the country opposed a large and expensive military establishment. The economic problems of the Great Depression further sapped the strength of the U.S. military. By 1939, the U.S. Army had been reduced, as General George C. Marshall put it, to that of a "third-rate power." The Army Air Corps was equally in disarray. General Henry H. Arnold stated that the Army's air arm had "plans but not planes."[9] This era was not auspicious for tactical innovation in the United States, especially in the field of aerial or airborne warfare.

The Italians actually led the world in this direction, having perfected the use of a static-line parachute and successfully dropped a paratroop unit during exercises in November of 1927. The Italians had also studied the techniques of using parachutes for logistical resupply and were the first to use them in 1928 to resupply the stranded crew of the airship *Italia* in the Arctic. However, the Italians experienced a slight setback when the head of their airborne force, General Guidoni, plunged to his death after a parachute malfunction. By the late 1930's, they recovered sufficiently to form several parachute battalions.[10]

In the early 1930's, the Russians were concerned about the Japanese invasion of Manchuria. During the modernization of their armed forces, Soviet military planners saw both the parachute and the transport plane as a perfect marriage and developed large-scale paratrooper units. The Russians continued to experiment and build upon their lessons learned. In September 1936, during the Belorussian Maneuvers, the Soviets displayed the ability to project paratroop forces over long distances. Many Western attachés viewed the drop with much interest.[11] Though the Soviets developed airborne units, they failed fully to exploit them during World War II. This lapse resulted from the principle that airpower is indivisible. The side with pronounced air superiority and with massive amounts of transport is the side in a position to use airborne forces. The Soviets lacked both for most of the war.[12] The Soviet airborne forces, a microcosm of the total Soviet force structure, suffered through many of problems that plagued the Red Army after Stalin's purges. Few senior commanders were readily capable of conducting strategic operations requiring the integration of airborne forces into the complex overall combat scheme of deep battle doctrine.[13]

Nevertheless, the ideas of Billy Mitchell slowly became a reality. But it was the Germans, and not the United States, who first capitalized on the Soviet maneuver experience. Soviet ideas gave Nazi Germany an appreciation for the strategic possibilities of paratroop units. While the Soviets were the first to publicly display a military parachute force, discreet work had been ongoing in Germany, where the Treaty of Versailles banned large-scale military development. A secret military clause in the 1922 Treaty of Rapallo enabled the Germans to attach liaison officers to the Soviet Army. Additionally, the Treaty of Versailles did not expressly prohibit Germany from possessing gliders or paratroopers. *Luftwaffe* pilots trained in gliders and became the first paratroopers, since it was determined that they were already accustomed to the air.[14] Within the *Luftwaffe*, and not within the Army, Germany found its airborne leader, General Karl Student.

The Germans initially envisioned three components to their airborne forces; parachute forces, glider forces, and air-landing forces. These forces were separate, but could be organized under a single commander to accomplish virtually any appropriate operation. The Germans were unique in that their airborne forces operated under *Luftwaffe* control. By January 1939, the Germans had created the 7th *Fliegerdivision* as part of their preparations for general war. As Germany prepared to unleash its offensive might, its future enemies continued to think primarily in terms of defensive land warfare behind the concrete walls of the Maginot Line.

The Germans displayed their ability to overcome static defense systems with vertical envelopment forces during their conquest of Western Europe in 1940. The combination of glider and paratroop units securing key bridges and airfields in Holland and Belgium in front of the German ground onslaught was vital to the success of blitzkrieg. A group of fifty-five German glider-borne troops neutralized the garrison of Fort Eben Emael, the key to the Belgium defense line along the Albert Canal. This underground fortress had been built to defy the heaviest possible ground attack, but was ill-suited for defending against airborne troops.[15] In the first hour at Eben Emael, a military revolution occurred with the addition of a vertical flank to the dimensions of the battlefield. Warfare changed to usher in an era of the highly skilled, all-around warrior.[16] The allied nations recognized the need for such troops and began to model their tactical capabilities and forces to match those of their German adversaries. However, an isolationist mood still persisted in the United States, even as President Franklin D. Roosevelt sought to draw his country into the reality of a coming war.

The U.S. was at the infant stage of developing its airborne capabilities, but German experiences were well documented and helped shape initial U.S. plans. Ironically on 25 June 1940, as the French were surrendering to Hitler in the railroad car in which they had received the German surrender in 1918, the U.S. Army officially assigned Major William C. Lee, the "Father of the Airborne," to the U.S. Army Airborne Project.[17]

Perhaps the greatest impetus for the rapid expansion of United States Army's airborne capabilities was the German invasion of the strategically important Mediterranean island of Crete in May 1941. The U.S. military attaché in Egypt, Major Bonner Fellers, wrote in his 1941 report on Crete that:

The drama of Crete marks an epic in warfare. The concept of the operation was highly imaginative, daringly new. Combat elements drawn from Central Europe moved with precision into funnel-shaped Greece. Here they re-formed, took shape as a balanced force, were given wings. The operation had movement, rhythm, and the harmony of a master's organ composition. On 20 May and succeeding days, this force soared through space; its elements broke over Crete in thundering crescendos – all stops out. For the first time in history airborne troops, supplied and supported by air, landed in the face of an enemy, and defeated him. [18]

The victory in Crete secured the southern flank of the German advance into the Mediterranean area. More so, it further demonstrated the power of the German blitz, this time in the capture of an island protected by two hundred miles of sea dominated by the Royal Navy. Yet, the cost in manpower, equipment, and resources was too much for Hitler to stomach. He was convinced that the Allies would forget about airborne forces. He felt that the surprise factor was gone and that the use of airborne forces in the future would prove too costly. He stated to General Student in 1941:

> Crete has proved that the days of the parachute troops are over. The parachute weapon is just nothing more than a weapon of surprise; the moment of surprise has worn out by now.[19]

It is interesting in retrospect to note that two nations could hold diametrically opposing views. Immediately following the invasion of Crete in 1941, both Germany and the United States moved in opposite directions with regard to the use of large airborne forces.

The Allies, specifically the United States, were very impressed with the ability of German airborne forces to conquer Crete in the face of British sea power and strong, well-prepared defenses. Major Fellers' concise report on the operation widely circulated in Allied military circles. Major General James Gavin, one of the original pioneers of the airborne concept, "avidly read" the reports of Fellers and remembers American officers reading and rereading them as well.[20] He became convinced that air mobility was absolutely essential if the Allies were ever to defeat the powerful German military machine.[21] Gavin himself, as a member of the West Point Department of Tactics, became deeply interested in the Germans' new arm, the parachute-glider troops. His access to many of the original documents on German airborne operations in Holland would further convince him of the utility of parachute forces.[22]

---

[1] James M. Gavin, *Airborne Warfare*. (Washington, D.C.: Infantry Journal Press, 1947) 175.

[2] United States Army White Paper, "Concepts for the Objective Force" (2002) 10, 12.

[3] United States Army White Paper, "Objective Force in 2015" (8 December 2002) 6.

[4] Gerard M. Devlin, *Paratrooper! The Saga of U.S. Army and Marine Parachute and Glider Combat Troops During World War II* (New York: St. Martin's Press, 1979), 2.

[5] Michael Hickey, *Out of the Sky: A History of Airborne Warfare* (New York: Charles Scribner's Sons, 1979), 9.

[6] Devlin, 22-23.

[7] Hickey, 14.

[8] John R. Galvin, *Air Assault: The Development of Airmobile Warfare* (New York: Hawthorn Books, Inc., 1969), vii.

[9] Maurice Matloff, "The American Approach to War, 1919-1945," in *The Theory and Practice of War*, ed. by Michael Howard (Bloomington, IN: Indiana University Press, 1975) 215-218.

[10] Hickey, 14.

[11] David M. Glantz, *The Soviet Airborne Experience*. (Ft. Leavenworth: Research Survey 5/Combat Studies Institute, U.S. Army Command and General Staff College, 1984) 8-13.

[12]Christopher Bellamy, *The Evolution of Modern Land Warfare.* (New York: Routledge, Chapman, & Hall Inc., 1990) 89.

[13]Glantz, 26.

[14]Maurice Tugwell, *Airborne To Battle: A History of Airborne Warfare 1918-1971.* (London: William Kimber and Co., 1971), 25-27.

[15]Trevor N. Dupuy, *The Air War in the West: September 1939 – May 1941* (New York: Franklin Watts, Inc., 1963), 19.

[16]James Lucas, *Storming Eagles: German Airborne Forces in World War Two.* (London: Arms and Armour Press, 1988), 23.

[17]Jerry Autry, *General William C. Lee: Father of the Airborne.* (Raleigh, NC: Airborne Press, 1995), 100.

[18]Bonner F. Fellers, Military Attaché Report, *Air-Borne Invasion of Crete* (Military Intelligence Division, War Department General Staff, Egypt: 9 August 1941) 1.

[19]Edward N. Luttwak, *The German Army of the Second World War. The Parachute Troops: the Fallschirmjaeger Formations* (Ft. Monroe, VA, 1983), 93.

[20]James M. Gavin, *On to Berlin.* (New York: The Viking Press, 1978) 1-2.

[21]Galvin, 60.

[22]James M. Gavin, *On to Berlin.* 1.

CHAPTER 2

THE FORMATIVE YEARS: 1940-1941

U.S. Airborne Force Development (pre-Crete Invasion)

Ironically, and coincidently, the first published United States Army doctrine, FM 100-5, which addressed airborne operations, was published on 22 May 1941, the day after the Germans began their invasion of Crete. The United States was in the infant stage of developing its airborne doctrine and organizations and the War Department's publication reflected this fact. The last official edition of FM 100-5 had been published in 1923, and it was superseded by a tentative 1939 version. Not until June 1944 would an updated version be published by the War Department to reflect wartime organizations and operations. It was with the 1941 version that the United States Army embarked upon the Louisiana maneuvers, and more importantly, the first two and a half years of World War II.[1]

The 1941 vision of paratroopers looked different on paper than as it appeared over the skies of Europe during World War II. FM 100-5 defined parachute troops as "troops moved by air transport and landed by means of parachute" and air landing troops as "troops moved by powered aircraft who disembark after the aircraft reaches the ground." The manual distinguished between the two types of troops since the capabilities were distinctly different and reflected the proposed use of parachute troops. "Ordinarily, parachute troops may be considered as the advance guard of air landing troops or other military or naval forces."[2] At no point did the field manual address gliders or organizations larger than a battalion.

Several missions for paratroopers included seizing, holding, or exploiting important tactical localities, executing an envelopment from the air in conjunction with an attack by ground forces, surprise attacks as a diversion or feint in support of other operations, or executing an attack against isolated enemy positions that were impossible or impracticable of attack by other ground forces.[3] Interpreted as limited objective in scope, the doctrine of the time maintained a raider-like quality. Parachute troops were to be subordinate to either a higher headquarters ground force or to an air-landing force. Parachute troops were merely a combat multiplier to other forces. Limited objectives equated to limited expectations of their utility.

The United States Army General Headquarters (GHQ) maneuvers in late 1941 reflected these beliefs. Though conducted after the operations in Crete had ended, the utilization of paratroopers reflected the pre-Crete United States doctrine. During phase 1 of the Louisiana operations, Company A, 502nd Parachute Infantry Battalion participated on the 'Blue' side. 127 soldiers parachuted into the 'Red' rear area on a suicide mission. No plan was ever developed to linkup the paratroopers with ground or air-landing forces. The action had little bearing of the ground operations being conducted but did succeed in distracting and embarrassing the Red Army.[4]

With another opportunity to prove their worthiness, the company became attached to the Red forces for phase 2 of the Louisiana maneuvers. The Red commander, General Lear, squandered an opportunity to use the parachutists to seize key bridges or road junctions. Instead, they were dropped 100 miles into the rear of the Blue forces. Once again, the paratroopers were a distracter, but otherwise did not hinder Blue force operations.[5]

During the Carolina maneuvers, the entire 502nd Parachute Infantry Battalion seized the airfield at Pope Field to allow an infantry battalion from the 2nd Infantry Division to air-land. The operation achieved surprise, but the defenders were able to rout the parachutists. The air-land operation continued despite the setback for the training benefit of all involved parties. The battalion later seized bridges in an operation not tied to any friendly scheme of maneuver.[6]

The maneuvers never provided a realistic test for the fledgling parachute forces. The four maneuver drops conducted seemed to indicate that parachute troops were most useful in small-scale sabotage activities. The airfield seizure operation at Pope Field seemed to indicate that paratroopers should be dropped some distance from their intended objectives to avoid being destroyed. LTC William C. Lee, the head of the U.S. Army Airborne Project, was disappointed with the missed opportunity to demonstrate the effectiveness of the paratroopers. One of only three battalions then active, the 502nd had spent much of its time preparing for the maneuvers, often neglecting other essential training requirements.[7]

At the time of the German invasion of Crete, the United States' airborne forces were minimal. The Airborne Test Platoon had validated the fact that the United States army could effectively conduct parachute drops from multiple aircraft formations. The Test Platoon pioneered equipment and training requirements, as well as basic tactics once on the ground. The initial groundwork for the emerging doctrine had been laid. Flush with the success of the Airborne Test Platoon, the 501st Parachute Infantry Battalion (PIB) was organized on 1 October 1940. The battalion's mission was to train and provide cadre for other airborne units as needed. The 501st was located at Fort Benning, Georgia and fell under the auspices of the Parachute Provisional Group formed 31 March 1941 and headed by LTC Lee. The Airborne Group took charge of the training, providing resources and oversight, organized the Army jump school, and prepared the Army for an expanded airborne force that was ready for war.[8] As the German Airborne forces were displaying their awesome capabilities in Crete, the United States Army consisted of a small training force, numbering a Group Headquarters and a single Parachute Infantry Battalion.

During the years leading to the U.S. entry into World War II, the rapid expansion of the military created demands on all services and branches, each competing with the other for priority of resources. More than any other soldier, the paratrooper relied on the U.S. Army Air Force (USAAF) for transportation. USAAF transport resources numbered slightly more than 100 aircraft and were strained to support the Army's training requirements.[9] The USAAF utilized three different aircraft to support airborne operations, the C-33, C-39, and B-18. The C-33 was the most widely used in the time leading up to May 1941 and was capable of carrying 12 paratroopers.[10]

From 1940-1942, paratroopers were equipped with the T-4 parachute.[11] The T-4 opened with a static line and had two visible differences from later variants. The main parachute was square and secured with three snap hooks. The reserve was rectangular, large, bulky, and worn vertically on the chest, thus leaving little room for additional equipment.[12] Paratroopers carried only a pistol and knife, dropping their weapons and other equipment in containers located under the wings of the aircraft. The use of weapons containers provided additional challenges for paratroopers once on the ground. Any failure to collect much-needed weapons would all but assure the destruction of any parachute force.

In May of 1941, the United States airborne effort consisted of a single parachute infantry battalion. The 501st PIB was infantry-centric and did not constitute a combined arms organization. Extremely limited in scope, the airborne doctrine envisioned small-scale operations in support of other ground operations. A general lack of understanding on behalf of senior Army ground commanders existed over the usefulness of airborne troops, as demonstrated in the Louisiana and Carolina maneuvers, which incidentally occurred after the Germans invaded Crete. USAAF resources lacked the numbers to support burgeoning missions across the entire Army, let alone to support a growing, albeit slowly, airborne concept. Paratroopers were jumping with a new parachute that did not allow them to carry their necessary equipment and weapons.

In essence, on the eve of the German invasion of Crete, the United States airborne concept was nothing more than a novelty going through the initial stages of testing and growth. The nation was not at war and thus lacked any real incentive to focus on efforts other than improving the quality of the existing force structure. The German use of airborne forces during the 1940 invasion of Western Europe had demonstrated the tactical possibilities of such units. What remained to be seen was the operational utility of a large airborne force. The United States was equipped neither doctrinally, ideologically, nor technologically for large-scale airborne operations, and most likely could just barely function in its current state. In order to spur rapid development conceptually, as well as materially, a demonstration needed to provide an impetus. The German Armed Forces provided just such an example in on 21 May 1941.

German Airborne Forces – May 1941

The German term for the paratrooper during World War II was *Fallschirmjaeger*. The term *Jaeger* described their tactical frame of reference. *Jaegers* were light infantry who used fluid, firepower-evasive, rather than firepower-dependent, tactics. They relied on surprise and initiative, rather than material means, to overcome their adversaries. Initially, the development of paratroopers proceeded separately within both the *Luftwaffe* and the Army. In late 1938, after a long battle between the two services of the *Wehrmacht*, the Germans made the decision to place all parachute troops under the sole command and responsibility of the *Luftwaffe*. This decision imparted a different operational orientation. The Army saw the paratroopers as mere tactical facilitators, to seize bridges, defiles, and the like to speed the movement of tank and mechanized formations. The *Luftwaffe* wanted a much broader role, an airborne equivalent to the Army's panzers.[13]

German airborne doctrine reflected both uses and potential operations were classified into two groups according to their purpose. The first took the form of sending an advance force by air to seize important terrain features, pass obstacles, and hold the captured points until the attacking ground forces arrived. These limited objective operations were successfully displayed before Crete at Eben Emael, Holland, and in

Greece; and unsuccessfully in the Ardennes in 1944. The second group was the operations having as their objective the capture of islands. The invasion of Crete demonstrated this on a large scale, and in 1943 on a smaller scale with the capture of Leros, a Greek Island in the Aegean Sea. Additionally, the Germans planned, yet never executed, an assault on the island of Malta.[14]

The Germans envisioned utilizing three different methods, either singly or in concert, to land troops from the air at their place of commitment; by parachute, via gliders, or by air-landed planes. All three methods were used throughout World War II in varied combinations, depending upon the situation. Inserting troops by parachute would allow the largest number to arrive at the same time within a certain area. The main disadvantages were that assembly and the locating of weapons containers was time consuming.

Gliders offered the greatest advantage in that they arrived quietly and deposited their whole load in one place. Troops could disembark within a manner of seconds, bringing their full fire and striking power to bear immediately. Gliders could also deliver weightier loads such as heavy weapons, artillery, trucks, and light tanks. Field Marshal Albert Kesselring, arguably one of the most successful German generals during World War II, was a big proponent of the use of gliders.

> I maintain that at least the same concentration of forces can be achieved with a glider landing as with a parachute jump. Experience shows that parachute landings are very widely scattered, so that assembly takes considerable time. Gliders, according to their size, hold ten to twenty or even more men, who immediately constitute a unit ready for combat.[15]

The major disadvantage of glider commitment lay in the fact that once used, they tended to clog the drop zone and could only be used once.

The final means of insertion called for the air landing of troops in transport aircraft. The advantages were similar to those of gliders, with the added factor of control that a powered aircraft offered. The success of landing and unloading troops hinged upon the guarantee of a sufficiently large landing zone. The Germans thus considered air-land operations unsuitable for the purpose of capturing an airhead, and instead emphasized their use during the expansion.[16]

The Germans preferred to execute the landing of paratroopers directly on their objectives. This method of employment would increase the level of surprise and immediately allow exploitation by the lightly armed paratroopers. For large operational drops, the German doctrine called for "oil spots," numerous drop zones, creating a number of small airheads, and no predetermined point of main effort. Paratroopers would then expand the airheads according to events as they unfolded.[17] As opportunities were developed, the most successful landings became the focus of the main effort. Friedrich August von der Heydte, a company commander during the Crete operation, summed up oil spot tactics as such:

> At first to attack at several places, creating several strongpoints on the ground from the air, in order to break apart the enemy's defensive zone from within, complicate the forming of a main defensive effort, and disrupt the communications necessary for the defensive. Then to shift the main effort of the attack to one of these strongpoints and reinforce this one strongpoint through the constant introduction of new forces (by air transport, which is why this one strongpoint had to be an airport). Finally to fortify this strongpoint and enlarge it in an oil spot-like manner until it reaches the other strongpoints, absorbing them. This 'oil spot method'…was given preference by the German side in independent

airborne operations over the 'carpet tactic' employed by the Allies...In Holland as well as in Crete the oil spot method stood the test.[18]

Though not at the forefront during the development of the airborne warfare concept, the Germans did lead the world in the development of airborne organizations. In 1941, General der Flieger Karl Student's XI *Fliegerkorps* served as the German airborne headquarters within the *Luftwaffe*. The XI Air Corps consisted of three separate air transport regiments, an airborne assault regiment, the *Luftlande Sturm* Regiment, and a parachute division, the 7th *Flieger* Division. The German army also created a specific air-land division, the 22nd Infantry Division that would be attached to the airborne during operations.[19]

The 7th *Flieger* Division consisted of three *Fallschirmjaeger* Regiments, each with three battalions and other combat and support units. The *Sturm* Regiment consisted of three battalions and was trained for both parachute and glider borne operations.[20]

The 22nd Infantry Division was only used once, in Holland, during an airborne operation. During the Crete invasion, the Division guarded the Ploesti oil fields and could not move to the Greek staging areas in time. The 22nd Division fielded two different sets of equipment. One set was for use in regular ground combat, the other for air-landing operations. A further consideration for special missions also limited this division's employment for employment in ground combat.[21]

The 5th Mountain Division replaced the 22nd Division for the Crete operation. Germany had used non-tactical air transport to fly mountain troops in Norway without prior preparation. For the Crete invasion, little preparation and training was devoted to the 5th Mountain Division prior to the air-landings, though the landings were extremely successful.

The *Luftwaffe* possessed two aircraft capable of delivering paratroopers to battle, the JU-52 and the HE-111. Exit was through a hatch on the floor of the HE-111, a fact that made the JU-52 the preferred aircraft for airborne operations. Soldiers could exit from the door at the rear of the JU-52, thus increasing the speed of the exit while decreasing the amount of dispersion on a drop zone.[22]

The JU-52, a tri-motor aircraft powered by BMW radial engines capable of producing 835 horsepower each, had an overall length of 62 feet and a wingspan of 96 feet. The aircraft's maximum speed of 172 miles an hour, and its range was nearly 700 miles. Full-span flaps made it ideal for airborne operations. The flaps enabled the JU-52 to take off and land on very short runways. Specifically, the aircraft could slow to the ideal speed of 120 miles an hour for a controlled exit for paratroopers.[23]

The JU-52 served as a multi-role aircraft for the *Fallschirmjaegers*. The JU-52 carried only thirteen soldiers for operational parachute missions, a limitation imposed for the need to include weapons containers in the payload, as well as to give the paratroopers more room inside the aircraft to exit properly.[24] The aircraft could carry eighteen combat equipped soldiers in an air-landing role, a role well suited for its capabilities. The JU-52's capability to slow its speed on landing to 59 miles per hour made it an ideal air-landing platform on short, improvised runways, or on landing areas cluttered by obstacles.

The JU-52 also served as the towing aircraft during glider operations. Normally it would tow a single DFS-230 glider, but was capable of towing three if required.

The Germans made great use of gliders as a part of their airborne capabilities. The Treaty of Versailles restrictions placed upon Germany forced pilots to train in gliders. This expedient, along with the fact that gliders had been a popular pastime in Germany for several years, meant that the *Luftwaffe* had an abundance of good pilots.

The Germans developed several gliders throughout World War II. During the invasion of Crete, the *Luftlande Sturm* Regiment used the DFS-230 light assault glider. Constructed of lightweight metal tubing covered in plywood and linen, the DFS-230 was inexpensive to produce, easy to fly, and easy to land. It incorporated several braking mechanisms including skids wrapped in barbed wire, parachute braking devices, and rockets in the nose to reduce the length of the landing run. The DFS-230 had a towing speed of 112 miles per hour and could descend in a spiral dive at speeds up to 180 miles per hour. Its greatest appeal was the fact that it could carry ten soldiers equipped with their weapons and equipment into a small area, unlike the paratroopers who were scattered upon landing and had to find their weapons containers before fighting as a unit.[25]

German parachutists employed two types of parachutes, the RZ-16 (*Rückenfallschirm Zwangsauslösung*) and the RZ-20 during their invasion of Crete. Both parachutes used extremely tight fitting harnesses and deployed automatically through the use of a static line attached to a wire cable strung within the fuselage of the delivery aircraft. The Germans felt that parachute harnesses had to be tight fitting in order not to cause injury by failing to distribute the strain of opening shock evenly across the body.[26]

All German parachutes attached to the jumper along the waist, which gave the parachutist no control during his descent. The suspension lines attached to a D-ring above the jumper's head and then connected to the waistband of the harness with rigging lines. The jumper could reach neither the suspension nor rigging lines and hung in a diagonal position facing downwards. The jumper then used his hands and legs to bring him into a good landing position in the direction of the wind drift.[27]

The RZ-16's tight harness had a major disadvantage. Besides its uncomfortable nature, the parachute's opening shock developed a need to adopt an abnormal exit procedure from the aircraft. German paratroopers stood at the exit door with their feet braced at the corners and head inclined slightly upwards. When it came time to jump, the parachutist used his hands and feet pushed hard against the fuselage to propel him into the aircraft's slipstream. Due to the tight harness and the need to have both hands free upon exit, the German paratroopers could not carry rifles or machine guns in their hands or beneath their harness straps.[28] The RZ-16 also proved to be difficult to remove once the jumper landed.

The RZ-20's first operational use occurred during the invasion of Crete. Although similar to the RZ-16, the newer model provided a welcome relief to parachutists. The new harness of the RZ-20 provided the jumper with four quick-release buckles for rapid removal. The ability of a jumper to free himself from his parachute proved most welcome when under enemy fire or while being dragged on the ground by the winds.[29]

The canopy colors of parachutes leading up to Crete were predominately white for parachutists and camouflage-patterned for equipment. The white canopy showed up easily once the paratrooper reached the ground, and served as a beacon for enemy fire. The invasion of Crete saw the utilization of parachutes with both types of colors. Officers generally jumped a camouflage parachute with a white-capped canopy for easy recognition.[30]

The limitations of parachute harnesses inhibited the *Fallschirmjaegers* from carrying weapons other than pistols, grenades, and a gravity knife during airborne operations. The gravity knife served the practical purpose of providing a means to extract themselves from their parachutes. The Germans developed weapon containers to hold rifles, machine pistols, and other weapons needed on the ground. The metal containers used a standard parachute or one of special design. The specially designed parachutes ensured a canister fall rate of 26 feet per second, as opposed to the *Fallschirmjaeger's* rate of descent of roughly 16 feet per second. This rate difference ensured that the needed equipment would already be on the ground once the paratroopers landed.[31] The physics of time, descent, and area also increased the risk of paratroopers not landing in close proximity to the containers.

The weapons containers were either loaded internally or affixed to special racks under the wings of the JU-52s. Recovery of the containers after a drop was critical as the paratroopers were virtually defenseless on the ground. The absolute necessity of finding the containers constituted a flaw within the German airborne procedures. Container loss, or enemy fire preventing their retrieval on the ground, shifted advantages from paratroopers to the defenders.[32]

This problem significantly affected German paratroopers during the invasion of Crete, and the *Fallschirmjaegers* paid a heavy price in casualties. Ironically, the Germans never adopted these lessons. As late as 1944, during the final German airborne operation in the Ardennes, the loss of weapons containers prevented the Germans from achieving their assigned tactical tasks.[33]

On the plus side, the Germans succeeded in developing a combined arms airborne division. Sound German doctrine reflected the role each unit (paratroop, glider, or air-land) would play in subsequent operations. The Germans possessed an effective command structure that ensured unity throughout planning and execution phases. Perhaps the greatest German weakness lay in their technology. Their parachute and harness placed significant reliance upon weapons containers, which subsequently increased risk to both soldiers and missions.

The German doctrine and airborne organization far surpassed that of the United States on the eve of the Crete invasion. The German Armed forces possessed a force that was capable of conducting forced entry operations in support of other ground forces, or independently, at least in untested theory. The Germans had organic to the force all relevant combat support and combat service support assets. The Germans possessed a model that any country in the world with the resources and necessary commitment could copy. All that remained was an application of the German capabilities to serve as both an example, as well as an impetus. The highest levels of leadership within the *Luftwaffe* worked to gain approval for such a demonstration. On the eve of Germany's planned invasion of Russia, Operation Barbarossa, Hitler granted approval for Operation Mercury, the invasion of Crete.

In May of 1941, it was apparent that the United States lagged far behind their future adversary with regard to airborne warfare (See Table 1). The U.S. limited objective doctrine paled in comparison to the larger scale decisive operation doctrine of Germany. The existing organizational structure of both countries reflected the doctrinal uses envisioned, with Germany possessing a large, combined arms force, and the U.S. a single, infantry pure battalion. Germany integrated gliders within the force while the U.S. had yet to begin experimenting with this means of delivery. Both possessed a similar type aircraft in payload for paratrooper delivery and utilized containers for weapons delivery. Both possessed parachutes that were ill suited for complex combat operations (See Table 1).

Conceptually, the Germans possessed an impressive force that would prove deficient in many areas in Crete. The legacy of the Crete operation for the U.S. is twofold. First, it provided an impetus for expansion and development. Second, and most importantly, it provided both operational and technical lessons. The U.S. capitalized on the lessons and overhauled both their attitudes and equipment. Germany lost its desire to continue large-scale operations and did little to improve upon its capability throughout the remainder of the war.

Table 1. U.S. and German Airborne Capability Comparison (May 1941)

Subject	U.S. - May 1941	Germany - May 1941
Doctrine	Limited Objective/Small Scale Saboteur/Raider-like Tactics	Large Scale Usage/ Decisive Ops Potential for Independent Ops
Organization	1 x Parachute Battalion (501st PIB) No Air-Land Trained Units	XI *Fliegerkorps* 7th Abn Div Sturm Glider Rgt. 22nd Air-Land Div 5th Mountain Div
Troop Transport	C-33/B-18 12xParatroops	JU-52 13xParatroops 18xAir-land Troops
Gliders	None	DFS-230
Parachutes	T-4	RZ-16 & RZ-20
Weapon Delivery	Containers	Containers
Fire Support	None	75mm, 105mm, & 150mm Recoilless 50mm & 80mm Mortar 37mm AT Wpn

---

[1]Christopher R. Gabel, preface to the 1992 reprint of the War Department's FM 100-5, *Operations* (Washington, D.C., US Government Printing Office, 22 May 1941).

[2] War Department. FM 100-5, *Operations*. (Washington, D.C., US Government Printing Office, 22 May 1941), 241.

[3]War Department. FM 100-5, *Operations,* 242-243.

[4]Christopher R. Gabel, *The U.S. Army GHQ Army Maneuvers of 1941* (Washington, D.C., Center of Military History, United States Army, 1991) 76-77.

[5]Ibid, 107.

[6]Ibid, 144, 160.

[7]Ibid, 191.

[8]Autry, 102.

[9]Ronald G. Boston, "Doctrine by Default: The Historical Origins of Tactical Airlift." Air & Space Power Chronicles, (Maxwell Air Force Base, Alabama, May/June 1983) 2.

[10]The Airborne Test Platoon had conducted their initial test jumps from the B-18 medium bomber and had identified that a more capable aircraft was needed for parachute operations.

[11]The development of the T-4 parachute was spurred by the Airborne Test Platoon. During their operations, they had used the Air Corps T-3 parachute. (Marshall Brucer, *A History of the Airborne Command and Airborne Center.* (Sharpsburg, Maryland: Antietam Nation Museum) 12.) The T-3 was a free-fall, ripcord-activated parachute that current regulations determined could not safely be used below 1,500 feet AGL. The Chief of Infantry had received a waiver to allow parachute training operations to occur below 1,500 feet, but not below 750 feet. Regardless of the altitude, the T-3 was identified as lacking in safety considerations and the development of a static-line parachute commenced.

[12]Carl Smith, Mike Chappell. *US Paratrooper, 1941-45*. (Oxford: Osprey Publishing, 2000) 31.

[13]Luttwak, 3-5.

[14]Department of the Army Pamphlet No. 20-232. *Airborne Operations: A German Appraisal.* (Washington, D.C., 1951) 2-3.

[15]Ibid, 11.

[16]Ibid, 16.

[17]Tugwell, 84.

[18]Luttwak, 57. Von der Heydte took command of the 6th Regiment (Fallschirmjaeger) in 1944. The Regiment was thrown against American troops in the Normandy bridgehead at *Utah* beach, earning the nickname *Lions of Carentan*. Suffering

heavy casualties in Normandy the Regiment was formed up with the first Army in the autumn in a defensive position on the Albert Canal. He commanded the reinforced battalion that made the valedictory demonstration by German airborne forces during the Ardennes offensive the following spring. Although badly wounded, von der Heydte insisted upon making the jump on this operation.

[19] Ibid, 14-16, 48.

[20] Ibid, 15-16.

[21] Department of the Army Pamphlet No. 20-232, 15.

[22] Ibid, 50.

[23] Lucas, 179.

[24] Tugwell, 84.

[25] Internet website by Greg Way, *Fallschirmjaeger 1936-1944*, www.eagle19.freeserve.co.uk. Accessed 23 March 2003. Though leery of information gathered on the internet, I have verified much of the information as being factually correct through other sources. This site is remarkable with regards to the equipment used by German paratroopers in World War II.

[26] Lucas, 178.

[27] Ibid, 177-178

[28] Ibid, 178.

[29] Way, *Fallschirmjaeger 1936-1944*, www.eagle19.freeserve.co.uk. Accessed 23 March 2003.

[30] It is interesting to note that rumors spread among German parachutists that the dye used in the camouflage-pattern affected the smooth opening of the parachutes, lowering the morale of the Fallschirmjaegers. Throughout the war, German parachute officers sought to demonstrate the rumor's falseness with no avail. Attempts to alter the basic color of white for personnel parachutes were abandoned. Lucas, 178 and Way, www.eagle19.freeserve.co.uk/parachutes.htm.

[31] Lucas, 178.

[32] Ibid, 178-179.

[33] Ibid, 148-149.

CHAPTER 3

THE INVASION OF CRETE

The German onslaught throughout the Balkans in early 1941 forced allied Greek, British, Australian, and New Zealand units in Greece back towards the Mediterranean. The Germans conducted a spectacular airborne assault to seize the bridge across the Corinth Canal to cut off the allies from escaping to the Peloponessus. However, the German operation failed in its primary objective, as British forces were able to escape across the bridge. Eventually, the allies fell back to Crete and Egypt. The Germans did demonstrate excellent ground and air coordination with close air support for the paratroopers. The Germans came away from the Corinth Canal with the idea that opposed parachute landings were feasible.[1] This perception would cost them dearly during their invasion of Crete.

Hitler had to decide Germany's next move. He had no overall plan for continuing operations into the Middle East. He was engrossed in planning for Operation Barbarossa and much of his Balkan plan had been improvised. Hitler's commanders took advantage of the fuehrer's divided attention to influence him to invade Crete. Hitler viewed Crete as a base from which aircraft could dominate the Balkans, southern Italy, Egypt, and the Suez Canal, a view that Winston Churchill also shared.[2]

Each of the men who advised Hitler on invading Crete had his own reasons for seizing the island. Hermann Goering, the *Luftwaffe* commander in chief, was anxious for a spectacular victory to erase the memory of the Battle of Britain. Air Generaloberst[3] Alexander Lohr feared that British bombers based from Crete could destroy the Ploesti oil fields. The Chief of the German General Staff, Generaloberst Franz Halder, felt that Germany needed Crete to dominate the eastern Mediterranean. General der Flieger Karl Student, the commander of the XI Air Corps, planned the operation and assured Hitler that his beloved airborne forces could take Crete.[4]

Meanwhile, German intelligence grossly underestimated the strength of the British garrison defending Crete. Intelligence held that, "there are no Greek troops in Crete," and that, "the British troops are a permanent garrison." The conviction held that "British troops which fled from the Peloponese have been brought to Alexandria." The Germans estimated the British forces on Crete at "3 battalions of infantry, 30 light tanks, 30 AA guns, 40 AA machine guns, (and) 9 coast defense guns."[5] In fact, the British forces numbered 27,500 soldiers with an additional 14,000 Cretan and Greek troops.[6]

The German plan called for assaults on the Maleme-Canea area at first light. After consolidation throughout the morning, secondary landings would be conducted at Retimo and Heraklion.[7] Original plans called for no less than seven simultaneous landings throughout the northern portion of Crete, a true example of Student's "Oil Spot" tactics. Lohr and von Richthofen both objected on the premise that air support could not be massed accordingly.[8]

Lohr served as the overall commander of the invasion (See Figure 1), with Student and von Richtofen in command of the land and air forces respectively. The actual attack sectors were allocated to three groups. Battle Group West, under Generalmajor Eugene Meindl, was to capture Maleme. Battle Group Centre, under Generalleutnant Wilhelm Suessmann, the commander of the *7th Fallschirmjaeger* Division, was assigned the Canea area. Battle Group East, under Generalleutnant Josef Ringel, was to assault Heraklion.[9]

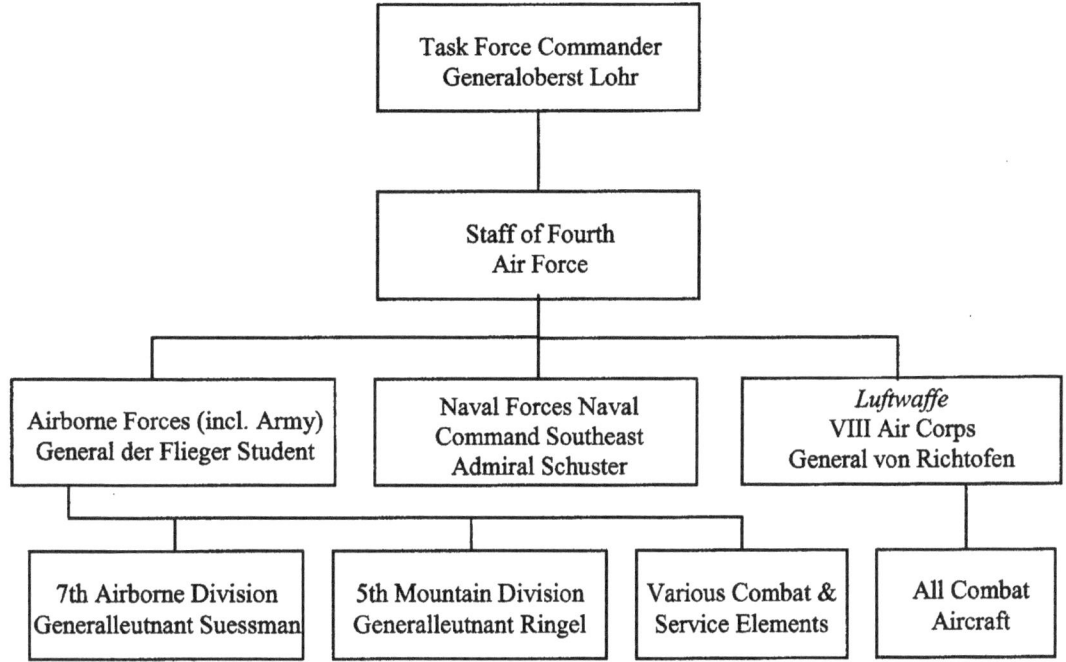

Figure 1. German Command Structure for Operation Mercury, adapted from Department of the Army Pamphlet No. 20-260, *The German Campaign in the Balkans (Spring 1941)*, (Washington, D.C., 1953), 142.

Preliminary German aerial bombardment of the British defenses began in early May. Daily, flights of two to three hundred planes struck the three airfields at Maleme, Retimo, and Heraklion. At sea, the *Luftwaffe* struck relentlessly against British warships, forcing the Royal Navy cease daylight operations around Crete.[10]

Early on the morning of 20 May 1941, waves of dive bombers and low flying fighter planes subjected the Maleme, Canea, and Suda Bay areas to heavy bombing and strafing attacks. At 0800, the first wave of German gliders landed near the Maleme airfield and the Canae beaches. Following closely behind were numerous JU-52s that began unloading their paratroopers (See Figure 2).

The German drop was inaccurate, with as detachments landing all over the Maleme area. Two of every three parachutes in each wave carried containers with weapons and supplies, and ferocious fighting broke out as the paratroopers attempted to locate their weapons. Around the airfield, the German paratroopers jumped into strong enemy fire from positions built into the hills south of the airfield. Many paratroopers were killed during the descent or on the ground shortly after landing.[11]

To compound the confusion during the early stages of the invasion, the paratroopers suffered devastating leadership casualties. The commander of the 7th *Fallschirmjaeger* Division, Generalleutnant Wilhelm Suessmann, was killed, along with a large portion of the division staff, when his glider crashed shortly after takeoff.[12] Generalmajor Eugene Meindl, commanding the Maleme group, was critically wounded shortly after landing and played no significant role during the invasion. Both the Maleme and Canea groups were therefore without their commanders.

The success of the Maleme operation depended on the quick capture of the airfield so that reinforcements could be landed without delay. To achieve this objective the British forces had to be dislodged from Hill 107, which dominated the airfield and surrounding terrain. A severe consequence of Meindl's wounds was a lack of central direction in the battle for Maleme and Hill 107.[13] At 1500, remnants of the initial force launched simultaneous attacks on the hill and the airfield. Despite heavy opposition and fire from the British antiaircraft guns emplaced near the airfield, the attackers captured

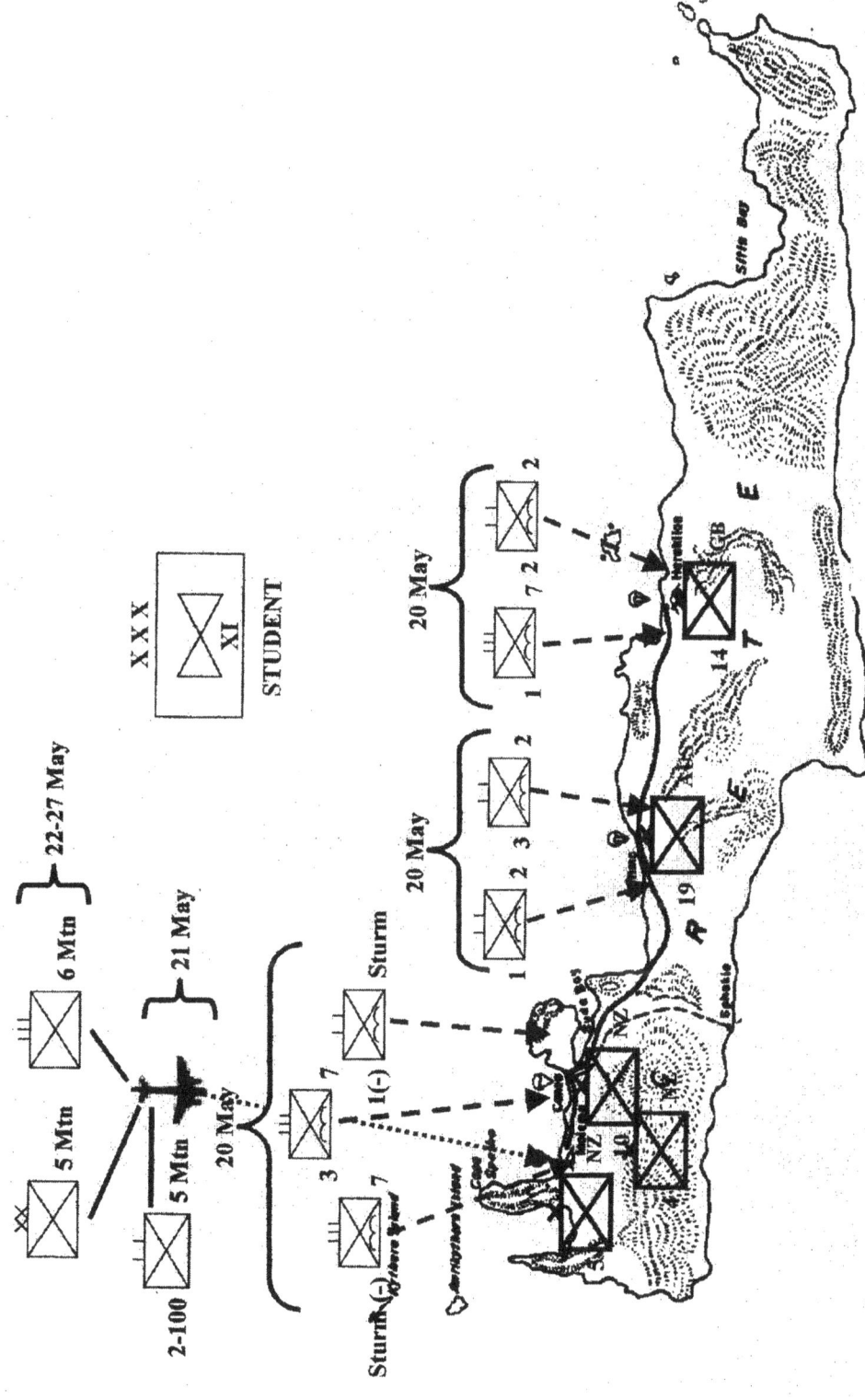

Figure 2. Assault on Crete. Base map from Department of the Army Pamphlet No. 20-260. *The German Campaign in the Balkans (Spring 1941)* Washington D.C., 1953), 122, Graphics by author.

the northern and northwestern edge of the airfield and advanced up the northern slope of Hill 107.

The Centre group, which was to capture the village of Suda and the town of Canea, landed on rocky ground and suffered many jump casualties. The few men who were not wounded attempted to gather weapons and ammunition and establish contact with their comrades. Small perimeters of paratroopers formed, but none were able to mount offensive operations.[14] The 10th New Zealand Brigade opposed the German paratroopers and engaged them with small arms and heavy weapons fire from olive groves that offered perfect camouflage for machine gun and sniper positions.

Meanwhile, the German command in Athens assumed from returning aircrews that the operation was progressing according to plan. The aircrews' reports showed that the preliminary bombardments and parachute drops had followed the planned time schedule and that losses in the air had not been too heavy. "My early impressions were that the start of the operation was favorable," Student told B.H. Liddell Hart during a post-war interview. However, "later reports were not so good."[15] On the initial assumption, which proved erroneous only after several hours had passed, troop carriers were readied for afternoon landings at Heraklion and Retimo.

The improvised airfields in Greece proved adequate for the morning lifts. But, the hot sun helped to intensify dust and haze as the second lift prepared to lift off. Delays in refueling caused flight programs to fall behind. Transport aircraft were not synchronized with the combat aircraft as in the morning lifts. The JU-52s arrived too late over the designated drop points and the paratroopers were therefore without direct fighter and bomber support.[16] The defenders suffered none of the initial shock effect, as had been the case in the Maleme area. Some of the German troops landed at the wrong points because the troop carriers had difficulty in orienting themselves. The haphazard and slow delivery of paratroopers onto the drop zones allowed the defenders to concentrate their fires on each wave of JU-52s.[17] Facing very heavy British fire, the parachutists suffered even more casualties than at Maleme and failed to capture the airfields, towns, or ports. After they touched ground, the Germans found themselves in an almost hopeless situation. Surrounded by greatly superior enemy forces, they struggled for survival.

Air reconnaissance and radio messages had meanwhile rectified the erroneous picture of the first landings in western Crete. By the evening of 20 May not a single airfield had been secured by the Germans. The most favorable reports came from Maleme, where the defenders were falling back from Hill 107 and their perimeter defenses around the airfield. To further complicate problems, crashed aircraft and gliders obstructed parts of the airfield. Therefore, none were available for the airlanding of the 5th Mountain Division, scheduled for 21 May.[18]

During the night of 20-21 May, a British light naval force broke through the German aerial blockade and searched the waters north of Crete. German Admiral Schuster thereupon called back the first naval convoy, which was approaching Crete under escort by an Italian destroyer. At dawn on 21 May, German planes sighted the British ships and subjected them to heavy air attacks. One destroyer was sunk and two cruisers damaged. At 0900 the waters north of Crete were cleared of enemy ships and

Schuster's convoy continued its voyage in the direction of Maleme. During the day German dive-bombers based at Skarpanto and Italian planes flying from Rhodes scored several hits on British ships in Crete waters, thereby preventing them from intercepting the Axis convoy. German troops on the island anxiously awaited the arrival of artillery, antitank guns, and supplies, but poor weather conditions so delayed the convoy that it could not reach the island before darkness.

When it finally sailed around Cape Spatha at 2300, a British naval task force suddenly confronted the convoy, which was destined for Suda Bay to land reinforcements and supplies. The British immobilized the Italian escort vessel and sank most of the motor sailors and freighters. Many German soldiers, most of them mountain troops, drowned. Sea rescue planes, however, picked up the majority of the shipwrecked. A second convoy was recalled to save it from a similar fate. No further seaborne landings were attempted until the fate of Crete had been decided.[19]

On the morning of 22 May, VIII Air Corps started an all-out attack on the British fleet, which then withdrew from the Aegean after suffering heavy losses. The battle between the *Luftwaffe* and the British Navy ended with a victory for German air power, which came to dominate the air and waters north of Crete.[20] This would serve as an important lesson for the U.S. in future operations. Air superiority would be vital for not only airborne, but for all operations.

On the morning of 21 May, a few planes were able to make crash landings on the beaches near Maleme with badly needed weapons and ammunition for assault troops in the area. New Zealand artillery fire interdicted any landing on the airfield proper. The

German response was to drop additional parachute troops behind enemy positions dominating the airfield.

Oberst Bernhard Ramcke assembled 550 paratroopers in Greece who had been left behind on the first day and formed a reserve battalion. He was ordered to jump west of Maleme airfield and assist in clearing British positions in its vicinity. Mountain infantrymen already seated in their transport planes were hastily unloaded and immediately replaced by Ramcke's men. In the early afternoon four companies of parachute troops jumped from low altitudes above the vineyards near Maleme. The two that were supposed to land behind enemy lines descended directly into well-camouflaged enemy positions and were almost completely wiped out. The other two joined the German assault troops in place, and by 1700, these forces succeeded in dislodging enemy infantry from the town of Maleme and the hills surrounding the airfield. German tactical air assets effectively supported the airdrop. However, German dive-bombers failed to silence British artillery pieces, which were particularly well camouflaged, and which, in order not to disclose their positions, held their fire whenever German planes were in sight.[21]

At 1600, troop carriers with the 5th Mountain Division troops began to land at Maleme airfield, even though the field was still under intermittent artillery and machine gun fire. Low-flying planes kept the defenders' fire to a minimum and the landings proceeded without major loss. A captured British tank was used as the prime mover to clear the airfield of damaged planes. As soon as the landing strip was cleared, planes landed and departed without interruption.

From this point on, reinforcements and supplies kept pouring in to seal the fate of Crete. Little by little the entire 5th Mountain Division was flown in. Even more important to the attack forces were the artillery pieces, antitank guns, and supplies of all types, which had been missing during the initial stage of the invasion, and which were now being airlifted into Maleme.

On 22 May, Generalmajor Julius Ringel, the commander of the 5th Mountain Division, assumed command of all German forces in the Maleme airfield. His first task was to establish contact with the Canea forces and to clear enemy troops from the western part of the island. For this purpose his mountain troops employed the same tactics they had applied so successfully at Mount Olympus and Thermopylae. By climbing along paths that were not even real trails and over heights previously considered insurmountable, the mountain troops, loaded with everything they needed to fight and sustain themselves, broke their own ground as they advanced. Then, they attacked the enemy in the flank or rear at points least expected. The Germans had no mules and were therefore forced to hand-carry their heavy weapons and ammunition across the rugged terrain. Throughout the struggle for Crete they adhered to their commander's motto that "sweat saves blood."[22] In heavy uniforms the mountain soldiers withstood days of scorching heat with temperatures rising up to 130 degrees Fahrenheit and nights at altitudes with temperatures below freezing that few could sleep.

On D+5, German mountain troops outflanked the British positions east of Maleme. On the next day, they entered Canea, the capital of Crete, and occupied Suda Bay after a forced march across the mountains. During this fighting the British offered strong resistance and showed no willingness to giving in. They made skillful use of the terrain and delayed the German advance using sniper and machine gun fires. Wire and minefields protected some of their positions.

While the struggle for western Crete was raging, German reconnaissance planes reported that a few British planes had returned to Heraklion airfield on 23 May and that reinforcements were arriving by sea in the eastern part of the island. For the *Luftwaffe* to maintain complete air superiority over Crete, the return of British planes en masse must be prevented with all means. The decision came to reinforce German troops in the Heraklion pocket by dropping hastily assembled parachute units. They were to take possession of the airfield and, until relieved by approaching ground forces, prevent the landing of British planes. Four companies of parachute troops were formed at Maleme and dropped in the vicinity of the Heraklion pocket west of the town. Immediately after landing 28 May, the parachute units contacted the embattled pocket force and launched a concerted attack against the British positions. With air support, the Germans eliminated several enemy strongholds. After regrouping his forces during the night, the German commander at Heraklion set out to capture the town and the airfield early the next morning. At daybreak the German troops closed in on the British positions. Not a shot was fired. British naval vessels had evacuated the Heraklion garrison during the preceding night.[23]

By this time British resistance had crumbled everywhere. German supplies and equipment were landed at Suda Bay without interference from enemy naval or air units. On 29 May, motorized reconnaissance elements, advancing through enemy-held territory, established contact with the German forces in the Retimo pocket and reached Heraklion the next day. On 30 May, a small Italian force that had landed two days earlier at Sitia Bay on the eastern tip of Crete, linked up with a German advance detachment.[24]

On 1 June, after repeated encounters with enemy rear guards, German forces reached the south coast of the island. Crete could be considered secure. Despite the long delay in the issuance of evacuation orders, the British Navy was able to embark approximately 17,000 men for Egypt. The Royal Navy has often rescued the British Army from tough predicaments, but seldom did it show more devotion than displayed on the four terrible nights of 28-31 May, while subjected to severe losses and constant harassment by German planes. It was a repetition of Narvik, Dunkirk, and the Peloponessus. Once more a British expeditionary force had been committed to battle without proper air cover.[25]

Meanwhile, the Germans had their own wounds to lick. Crete had been a sobering experience. Expectations for a quick victory had faded in the face of prolonged combat against a tenacious adversary. Combat realities had no added up to the sum of the airborne promises, and the Germans would never attempt such and audacious airborne operation again. However, outsiders who were not privy to the German airborne realities might honestly conclude that Crete had been an unalloyed success.

There remains no consensus among historians as to the total amount of casualties suffered by both sides. German after action reports list total casualties between 3,986 and 6,453 men, though Winston Churchill stated that more than 4,000 graves were counted around Maleme, and another 1,000 at Retimo and Heraklion.[26] Other reports list German losses among the airborne forces as 3,250 killed or missing, and 3,400 wounded from the 7th Division, and 700 killed from the *Sturm* Regiment alone.[27] Some 350 aircraft, over half of which were JU-52s, were lost or heavily damaged.[28]

The British lost over 4,000 men killed or missing, 2,500 wounded, and left behind 12,000 troops that were eventually captured. The British lost all their war material on Crete, nine warships were sunk and seventeen were damaged, including the fleet's only aircraft carrier, and lost 46 aircraft of all types.[29]

---

[1] Hickey, 59.

[2] Galvan, 46.

[3] I am using the German Army and *Luftwaffe* ranks for historical purposes. The rank equivalents are as of May 1941 and were found in Maurice Tugwell's, *Airborne To Battle: A History of Airborne Warfare 1918-1971*. (London: William Kimber and Co., 1971), Appendix 1, 354.

[4] Galvan, 46.

[5] Bonner Fellers, Military Intelligence Division, War Department General Staff, Military Attaché Report: Egypt, Subject: Air-Borne Invasion of Crete (9 August 1941) 2.

[6] Department of the Army Pamphlet No. 20-260. *The German Campaign in the Balkans (Spring 1941)*. (Washington, D.C., 1953) 123.

[7] Hickey, 62

[8] Alan Clark, *The Fall of Crete* (London: Cassell & Co., 1962) 51.

[9] Tugwell, 86-87.

[10] Trevor N. Dupuy, *The Air War in the West: September 1939 – May 1941* (New York: Franklin Watts, Inc., 1963) 71.

[11] Department of the Army, *German Campaigns in the Balkans (Spring 1941)*, 129-130.

[12] Clark, 62-63.

[13] Lucas, 50-53

[14] Ibid, 56.

[15] Clark, 65.

[16] Department of the Army, *German Campaigns in the Balkans (Spring 1941)*, 132.

[17] Tugwell, 99.

[18] Clark, 98-99.

[19] Hickey, 68-71.

[20] Tugwell, 113.

[21] Ibid, 110.

[22] Clark, 100.

[23] Department of the Army, *German Campaigns in the Balkans (Spring 1941)*, 137.

[24] Ibid, 139.

[25] Hickey, 72

[26] Winston S. Churchill, *The Grand Alliance.* (Boston: Houghton Mifflin Company, 1950) 301. It is of interest to note that three of the German paratroopers killed at Crete were descendants of the Blucher family. The old and famous military family dynasty that had fought against Napoleon and had served Germany throughout the centuries, came to an end on Crete. Poppel, 67.

[27] Lucas, 58.

[28] Department of the Army, *German Campaigns in the Balkans (Spring 1941)*, 141.

[29] Tugwell, 113.

CHAPTER 4

THE EXPANSION YEARS: 1941 – 1943

Immediately following the operations in Crete, American planners, unaware of the true extent of the casualties suffered by the Germans, and focused only on the strategic results, began to rethink the utility of paratrooper units. LTC Lee, perhaps remembering the sobering conclusions made at the end of the GHQ maneuvers, remarked wryly, "After this successful operation, I think it would indeed be dull of us to say that parachute troops will seldom be employed in units larger than a battalion."[1]

Doctrine is something of a philosophy for military operations. It underlies policies and attitudes that often are unintelligible without knowledge of the doctrine upon which they are based.[2] However, the United States Army lacked clearly defined airborne doctrine, and its absence posed problems. Because the airborne program was the product of the Army Ground Forces and the Army Air Force, any doctrinal conflicts of divergences between them would naturally be reflected in attitudes and policies affecting the airborne effort.

Meanwhile, the apparent German success during the airborne invasion of Crete "convinced the last of the diehards that there was something to it besides showmanship."[3] This conviction led to greater activity in the formation of realistic and workable doctrine on behalf of American planners.

A conference was held on 8 April 1942 to consider drafts that the War Department G-3 had prepared as statements of policy. With some minor changes, the following statement later appeared as a War Department memorandum.

> An airborne operation is carried out by a task force of the combined arms organized by a theater or other higher commander. Plans for such an operation must give primary consideration to the air situation. This involves relative air strength, location of emplaning and deplaning points, protection of these points and the transports while enroute to the objective, and the air attacks at the objective in support of the landing.[4]

In May 1942, the Army published Field Manual (FM) 31-30, *Tactics and Technique of Air-Borne Troops*. At the time, it remained difficult to say how parachute troops would perform, since no American airborne troops had as yet participated in any combat operation. Much of the publication proved valid in tests; however, fundamental statements of doctrine were outside the scope of the field manual and the area remained void for the time being.[5]

Parachute troops were considered "the spearhead of a vertical envelopment, or the advance guard element of air landing troops or other forces" as previously noted. FM 31-30 listed a whole series of other possible objectives for parachute troops: seizing river and canal crossings as well as defiles; establishing bridgeheads; seizing or destroying vital enemy supply and communication installations; and creating confusion and acting as a diversion to the operations of the main force. Though these possible uses were not specifically defined in FM 100-5, their scope did reflect the concepts envisioned in pre-Crete thinking, as well as in practice during the GHQ maneuvers. However, FM 31-30 did reflect a significant evolution of capabilities in the following additional possible objectives: seizing and holding key terrain in the rear of organized beach defenses in conjunction with ground or naval operations; attacking defended position in the rear or flank, or landing within and attacking the interior of a highly organized perimeter defense; assisting ground offensives by means of vertical envelopment and subsequent seizure of important terrain and vital enemy establishments; and operating in conjunction with armored forces by consolidating and holding gains made by those units until the arrival of other friendly forces.[6]

Following German operations in Crete, the United States began a rapid expansion of its airborne organizations. The operation had a profound impact on the Army Chief of Staff, General George C. Marshall, and the War Department General Staff. Crete appeared to serve as the quintessential example of vertical envelopment. For the U.S. Army, Crete, more than any other single factor proved that airborne forces were "here to stay" and led Marshall to initiate plans to field a substantial number of American airborne forces.[7] Drawing upon the 501st Parachute Infantry Battalion (PIB) as cadre, three more parachute battalions were created: the 502nd PIB on 1 July 1941, followed closely by the 503rd PIB on 15 July 1941, and the 504th PIB on 5 October 1941. Additionally, two experimental air-landing battalions were established, the 550th Infantry Airborne Battalion (IAB) on 1 July 1941, and the 88th IAB on 10 October 1941.[8]

Expansion did not end with the creation of separate airborne battalions. Following the Japanese attack on Pearl Harbor, Marshall authorized the creation of Parachute Infantry Regiments (PIR), each composed of three parachute battalions. Within the first six months of 1942, six parachute regiments were created, with the cadre drawn from the four existing parachute battalions.[9] The 502nd PIR was activated on 3 January 1942, the 503rd and the 504th PIR on 24 March 1942, the 505th, 506th, and the 507th PIR on 25 June 1942.[10]

With airborne expansion in full swing, Marshall decided to create two airborne divisions immediately, the 82nd and the 101st, with more to follow in the near future. The 82nd had gained a great reputation during World War I after having spent more consecutive days in the line than any other American Division.[11] The division was reactivated in February of 1942 and went through numerous transformations in the following months. The 82nd began training initially as a conventional infantry division, then was converted to a motorized division, and finally designated as the 82nd Airborne Division on 15 August 1942.[12]

The 101st Airborne Division, a new division, also officially activated on 15 August 1942. Following the 101st were the 11th Airborne Division on 25 February 1943, the 17th Airborne Division on 15 April 1943, and the 13th Airborne Division on 13 August 1943.[13] When the Germans had invaded Crete, the United States Army had only a single Parachute Infantry Battalion on active duty. Two short years later, on the eve of the Allied invasion of Sicily, the United States Army had grown to four airborne divisions, with the fifth activated one-month later.

Throughout the newly activated 82nd Airborne Division's training period, shortages of transport aircraft, gliders, and parachutes were a continued hindrance. As late as March 1943, an inspection revealed "insufficient training in the field" and a need for "maneuver training" before the division could be certified as "fully prepared for combat duty."[14] To further complicate training matters, the 82nd faced organizational changes during its training period.

To fill the ranks of the 101st Airborne Division, this division drew half of its soldiers from the 82nd.[15] After the split, the 82nd retained the 325th and 326th Airborne Infantry Regiments, both glider regiments of two battalions each, and the 504th Parachute Infantry Regiment, which had been activated at Fort Benning, Georgia only a few months earlier.[16]

On 12 February 1943, about a month before the 82nd sailed for North Africa, the division went through yet another change in organization. Instead of two glider and one parachute regiments, the complement would be reversed, two parachute and one glider regiments. The 82nd lost the 326th, which would eventually join the 13th Airborne Division, and gained the 505th Parachute Infantry Regiment. As General Ridgway looked back upon the ordeal after the war, he was "convinced that no division that left the States for battle, either in Europe or the Pacific, had been torn up and put back together again so frequently or so drastically" as the 82nd Airborne Division. In his opinion, the changes in organization had left the division with about a third of the amount of training that other infantry divisions slated for overseas movement received.[17]

If the training the division conducted lacked the needed substance, so to did the training by the fledgling Troop Transport Command. Yet, this aspect was crucial:

> It goes without saying that the high demands made on the air arm in an operation by airborne troops are only within the capacity of a support air fleet which in organization and tactical employment is most carefully coordinated with the ground forces. It must, therefore, be conceded that an air arm constructed purely for long-range bombing is hardly in a position to cooperate successfully in a major operation by airborne troops.[18]

By November 1941, as airborne organizations were expanding, the Army Air Forces had yet to drop more than a company at a time and had rarely been able to conduct such operations successfully. The Army Air Forces suffered from an extreme shortage of transport planes and pilots (See Table 2). Driven by an urgent need for fighters and bombers, the Army Air Forces relied heavily on the belief that transport aircraft could be bought "off the shelf." This policy proved difficult to pursue, as exactly five transports were delivered in the last half of 1940, for a total of 122 transports of all types, mostly obsolete, by the end of the year. Throughout 1941, total delivery equaled only 133 transport aircraft. It was hardly surprising that the Army Air Forces could not supply a dozen aircraft for airborne training and strained its resources to provide 39 transports for the Carolina Maneuvers in November 1941.[19]

The need for transport aircraft to support the Army's ongoing mobilizations further aggravated the demands for the limited numbers. The civilian DC-3 airliner could easily be adapted for both logistics and troop carrier roles. The first DC-3s, now designated as the C-47, were received in September of 1941.[20] Its arrival made obsolete all other transport aircraft in use at the time for airborne operations. The C-53, similar to the C-47 with the exception of not being adaptable for carrying cargo, also arrived.[21]

Table 2. Number of C-47s Procured by Army Air Forces: Jan 1940-Dec 1945

Type & Model	1940	1941	1942	1943	1944	1945	TOTAL
C-47 Skytrain	115	165	1,057	2,595	4,900	1,536	10,368

Note: Procurement data represents the factory acceptances or receipt of legal title by resident factory representative of procuring agency. Totals include all aircraft procured by the Army Air Forces regardless of subsequent distribution to Army, Navy, recipients of lend-lease, or others. *Source*: Headquarters, U.S. Air Force, *Army Air Forces Statistical Digest* (Statistical Services, June 1947), 100.

The C-47 carried a normal payload of two and one-half to three tons, or eighteen combat equipped paratroopers. The aircraft could take off fully loaded from a dirt strip less than 1,000 yards long and external fuel tanks allowed nonstop flights of 1,500 miles. The C-47 could maintain cruising speeds of 150 miles an hour, as well as slow to 110 miles an hour or less, while remaining stable during airborne operations. The single door on the aircraft's port side measured eighty-four inches wide,[22] allowing convenient exits. More importantly, its door size facilitated exits by paratroopers loaded with weapons and equipment.

To transport or drop one parachute battalion would require roughly fifty aircraft; a regiment would fill about one hundred and fifty. Very large-scale operations would require hundreds, or even thousands, of aircraft.[23] To meet this demand, transport units expanded rapidly as well. The Army Ground Forces created the Troop Carrier Command in 1942, with all subordinate units designated as "Troop Carriers." The airborne mission of the troop carrier units served as their primary mission. All airfreight missions within theaters would be accomplished by troop carrier units temporarily attached to the theater air service command. In reality, unanticipated and overwhelming demand for air transport by both air and ground forces overseas often diverted the troop carriers from their primary task.[24]

The glider was potentially a solution to the shortage of aircraft. The United States, familiar with the role that German glider troops played during the invasion of the Low Countries, studied German actions in 1940. However, the War Department attributed German success at Eben Emael not to the men of the German glider force, but to the blitzkrieg of tanks and dive-bombing attacks. Thus, the potential value of a glider-borne force was lost in a fog of misinterpretation and American planners took little notice.[25] If the actions in Belgium left doubts about the utility of a glider force, the invasion of Crete removed them.

The United States began design and development for the Waco CG-4A glider. The demand for aircraft of all types swamped the aircraft industry and glider production was deliberately placed outside f the aircraft industry – with furniture firms in Michigan and with piano makers across the country.[26] Constructed with a fabric-covered tubular metal frame, the Waco could carry fifteen troops, 3,750 pounds of cargo, a jeep, antitank gun, or artillery piece. The whole nose of the glider opened upwards permitting easy loading.[27] Its biggest advantage, and one not lost on airborne planners, lay in its ability to deposit a complete squad of soldiers on the ground closely together, eliminating the assembly delay common to paratroopers. Some paper studies envisioned one C-47, fully loaded with paratroopers, having the capability to tow one or two gliders into combat, thus increasing effectiveness, substantially reducing the requirement for C-47s, and making airborne warfare more cost-effective.[28]

Many different types of gliders were turned out during World War II: bomb, power, training, and combat, for a total of 15,697 units. The overwhelming majority was troop carrying combat gliders; almost all of them were the CG-4 design (see Table 3).

Table 3. Total Number of Gliders Procured by Army Air Forces, 1940-1945

	1940	1941	1942	1943	1944	1945	TOTAL
Gliders	0	4	1,601	6,243	4,410	3,439	15,697

Source: Irving B. Holley Jr., *United States Army in World War II - Special Studies. Buying Aircraft: Materiel Procurement for the Army Air Forces* (Washington, D.C.: Office of the chief of Military History, Department of the Army, 1964), 373.

Attention to gliders did not obscure the fact that the T-4 parachute would not meet the demands expected of paratroopers in combat. Not having individual weapons with a paratrooper upon landing was unacceptable. In 1942, the Army fielded the T-5 static-line parachute. The T-5 was a round parachute with a smaller reserve located horizontally on the jumper's chest. The new reserve enabled other equipment to be carried beneath it, thereby eliminating the need for individual weapons containers. A paratrooper could also control his direction and rate of descent by pulling on the risers connected to the harness.[29]

It was decided that a parachute artillery battalion would support each parachute regiment and that a glider artillery battalion would support each glider regiment. To provide fire support during airborne operations, the airborne command tested three different howitzers. The 75-millimeter (mm) pack howitzer weighed only thirteen hundred pounds and had a maximum range of 9,475 yards. The 75-mm could be further broken down into nine separate components, making it ideal for parachute operations.[30]

Recognizing the limitations of the 75-mm, airborne units adopted the "infantryman's cannon," a standard 105-mm cannon with a sawed off barrel. The weapon weighed twenty-four hundred pounds and had a maximum range of 8,000 yards.

However, it possessed many limitations. Its shortened barrel detracted from its range, thus making it vulnerable to counter-battery fire. The howitzer could barely fit inside a glider, with the barrel projecting forward into the cockpit between the pilot and copilot. Additionally, the standard jeep lacked the ability to tow the gun on rough terrain, just barely capable on firm, relatively flat terrain. These shortcomings led to the acceptance of a battalion's worth of artillery, twelve standard 105-mm tubes with two and one-half ton trucks that would accompany an airborne division's rear support units. Once these howitzers linked up with the airborne assault forces, they would substitute for the shortened barreled version.[31]

The airlift required to transport a battalion of parachute or glider artillery was significant. Nine C-47s were required to lift a four-gun howitzer battery, and a total of 36 aircraft were needed for each parachute artillery battalion. Each glider could carry one howitzer or one jeep. The artillery system and their prime movers, combined with associated ammo trailers and personnel, would utilize an even greater number of C-47 transport aircraft.[32]

U.S. airborne forces on the eve of commitment to combat reflected all the growing pains of a new concept hurriedly grafted on to armed forces that were themselves subjected to serious growing pains. Organizations grew like tree houses, and equipment, when not in short supply, was adopted and discarded at a dizzying rate. Little doctrine existed, and organizational growing pains and a distant, but not wholly clear, German precedent heavily influenced what did exist.

[1] Devlin, 107.

[2] Chief of Military History, SSUSA. *The Airborne Team, 1941-1945*, 146.

[3] Interview with Brigadier General Frederick S. Borum, Commanding General, I Troop Carrier Command, and Colonel Reed Landis, Chief of Staff, I Troop Carrier Command, 11 July 1943. Air Force Historical Office, 253.85-2,

[4] Chief of Military History, SSUSA. *The Airborne Team, 1941-1945*, 146.

[5] Ibid, 148.

[6] War Department. FM 31-30: *Tactics and Technique of Air-Borne Troops*. (Washington, D.C., US Government Printing Office, 20 May 1942) para. 41-42.

[7] Clay Blair, *Ridgway's Paratroopers: The American Airborne in World War II*. (New York, Doubleday & Company, Inc., 1985) 29.

[8] Ibid, 532.

[9] Ibid, 32.

[10] Ibid, 533.

[11] Ridgway, 51. A few of the famous WWI 82nd veterans include Medal of Honor winner SGT Alvin York, and WWII Medal of Honor recipient, General Jonathon Wainwright, then a Major who served as a battalion commander during WWI.

[12] T.B. Ketterson, *82nd Airborne Division in Sicily and Italy: 9 July 1943, 13 Sep 1943, 22 Jan 1944* (82nd Airborne Division Official History, No publisher, 1943-1945) 1.

[13] Blair, 517, 519, 526.

[14] Albert N. Garland, Howard M. Smyth, and Martin Blumenson. *The Mediterranean Theater of Operations: Sicily and the Surrender of Italy* (Washington, D.C.: Center of Military History, United States Army, 1986) 93.

[15] Ridgway, 61. It is interesting to note how the 82nd and 101st came to an agreement as to which units and soldiers the 82nd would retain and which they would lose. MG Gavin refused to send "goof-offs and screwballs" to his old friend MG Bill Lee, the new commander of the 101st. Ridgeway took all the ranks and skills of the 82nd and divided them into two equal halves. The two generals then flipped a coin and the winner chose which half he wanted.

[16] Ketterson, 2.

[17] Ridgway, 61-62.

[18] F.O. Miksche, *Paratroops* (New York: Random House, 1943) 185.

[19] John C. Warren, *Airborne Missions in the Mediterranean, 1942-1945* (Maxwell AFB, AL: USAF Historical Division, Research Studies Institute, 1955) 1.

[20] Boston, 2.

[21] Warren, 2. Throughout WWII in the European Theater of Operations, no other aircraft other than the C-47 or C-53 dropped paratroopers or towed gliders into hostile territory in support of American operations.

[22] Headquarters, U.S. Air Force, *Army Air Forces Statistical Digest* (Statistical Services, June 1947) 100. Operations in Sicily would also prove the C-47 was extremely rugged. Shot full of shell and bullet holes, the aircraft held together. A two engine aircraft, it could stay aloft for a hundred miles with only one engine operational.

[23] Blair, 26.

[24] Warren, 3. It remains unclear whether or not the troop transport buildup also suffered from a prejudice to other Army Air Forces projects such as bombers.

[25] C.V. Glines, "Troop Carriers of World War II," *Air Force Magazine*, February 1999. Vol. 82, No. 2 [magazine online]; available from http://www.afa.org/magazine/Feb1999/0299troop.html; Internet accessed 31 March 2003.

[26] Irving B. Holley, Jr. *United States Army in World War II - Special Studies. Buying Aircraft: Materiel Procurement for the Army Air Forces.* (Washington, D.C.: Office of the chief of Military History, Department of the Army, 1964) 373.

[27] Tugwell, 134-135.

[28] Blair, 28.

[29] Smith, Chappell, 31-32.

[30] Blair, 41.

[31] Ibid.

[32] Ibid.

CHAPTER 5

THE U.S. AIRBORNE IN ACTION – OPERATION HUSKY

It was the first big-scale mass parachute drop in history, the testing and the proving of a bold new form of warfare which German operations against Crete had so dramatically and brilliantly inaugurated. It was the assault from the skies which men had dreamed of for generations.[1]

In 1943, Allied planners began preparations for an invasion into the soft underbelly of the Axis powers. British and American Generals agreed that Italy provided their best opportunity. At the time, Italian troops were performing nearly all occupation duties in Italy and the Balkans. If Italy could be forced to capitulate, Germany would be forced to commit large numbers of troops to hold their southern lines.

British Field Marshal Sir Alan Brooke, the Chief of the Imperial General Staff, felt that the Allies were not strong enough to conduct a direct assault from North Africa to the Italian mainland. He recommended several key islands in the Mediterranean whose capture might lead to the downfall of Rome's shaky fascist regime. Two of the islands immediately adjacent to mainland Italy that he recommended were Sardinia and Sicily.[2]

President Roosevelt, Prime Minister Winston Churchill, and the Combined Chiefs of Staff agreed at the ten day Casablanca Conference in January 1943 that Sicily would be the objective.[3] Roosevelt and Churchill believed that Sicily's capture would lead to the collapse of Italy, imposing a heavier strategic burden on Germany, and thereby providing additional assistance to the Russians on the Eastern Front.

Sicily is the largest island in the Mediterranean Sea. Triangular in shape, it measures 9,815 square miles. Separated from the "toe" of the Italian peninsula by only a two-mile expanse of water, the island virtually extends the mainland of Europe nearly a hundred miles closer to North Africa. Similar to Crete, some four hundred miles to the east, the terrain of Sicily favored a defending force. Hills and mountains cover the entire island except for gentle, sandy shores and small areas around Catania in the east and Gela in the south. A good road network made possible rapid movement of centralized reserves to any threatened point of the island's shoreline.[4] Mussolini, speaking at the 1937 Italian maneuvers, boasted, "Sicily is so well defended on the land, at sea, and in the air that it would be a nameless folly for anyone to try to invade her."[5]

Sicily would not be the first application of airborne warfare by the United States. However, it would be the first large scale airborne employment to support larger bodies of combat troops engaged in conventional ground warfare. Sicily also marked the first test of the airborne division concept, adopted by the United States less than a year earlier. The 82nd Airborne Division drew the American invasion force's most dramatic assignment.

The proposal called for a direct airborne attack on beach defenses. The 82nd Airborne Division sent a series of letters to the U.S. Seventh Army commander, MG George S. Patton, arguing against this mission for paratroopers. Lightly armed, they could neutralize only a limited area, while their appearance would reveal the exact location of the impending landing. Moreover, the paratroopers themselves would be exposed to naval bombardment of the beaches.[6] A mission some miles inland attacking Axis local reserves and securing key terrain seemed more appropriate. Once the idea of a direct attack plan was discarded, paratroopers would land behind the defenses, followed closely by an amphibious assault.[7] The U.S. Seventh Army would land on three beaches in the vicinity of Gela with the 1st, 3rd and 45th Infantry Divisions.[8]

The mission of the 82nd Airborne Division called for a Regimental Combat Team (RCT) to conduct a parachute assault on the night of D-1, 9 July 1943, to support the landing of the American 1st Infantry Division. The identified RCT, the 505th PIR,[9] reinforced with the 3rd Battalion, 504th PIR, was directed to drop on predetermined Drop Zones (DZs) near Gela, Sicily. The 504th PIR would be prepared to drop behind friendly lines on the night of D-Day to act as a supporting ground unit of the 505th PIR. The glider regiment, the 325th AIR, would be prepared to land in Sicily on call after the night of D-Day, following cessation of enemy air resistance.[10] All proposed airborne operations were limited by an acute shortage of troop transport aircraft and gliders that made a mass jump of the 82nd impossible.[11]

The 505th RCT planned to drop several hours before the landing of the 1st Infantry Division (See Figure 3). The primary mission was to prevent the movement of enemy units south through the town of Niscemi toward the landing beaches near Gela. It was hoped that the 1st Infantry would relieve the 505th RCT sometime during D-Day.[12]

The 3rd Battalion, 504th PIR would drop three miles south of Niscemi at approximately 2320 hours and defend the high ground in vicinity of its DZ. Additionally, the regiment would block the two main roads leading south from Niscemi, act as an advance guard for the RCT, and patrol the area adjacent to the battalion position.[13]

The 2nd Battalion, 505th PIR would drop south of Nescemi at approximately 2400 hours to defend the high ground at the western half of the DZ and establish roadblocks on the secondary roads to the west leading towards Gela. The RCT headquarters and the 1st Battalion, 505th PIR would follow the 2nd Battalion at 0012 hours. 1-505th PIR would defend the eastern half of the DZ, and on order, dispatch two companies to seize the main road junction 500 yards south of the DZ.[14]

The 3rd Battalion, 505th PIR would drop just south of the road junction and defend the high ground in its area, patrol to the east, and send one platoon to start a signal fire behind the landing beach as a guide to the 1st Division conducting an amphibious assault.

A demolition section would drop to the west of 3-505th PIR and destroy railroad and highway bridges.[15]

Two batteries of the 456th Parachute Field Artillery Battalion (PAFB) would drop with the battalion combat teams, move to firing positions identified on aerial reconnaissance photos, and prepare to fire on selected road junctions, enemy strong points, and avenues of approach leading to the defended areas.[16]

The mission assigned to the 505th RCT was a practical airborne mission and the plan was sound. The timing of the operation, however, left much to be desired. It called for a quarter moon that would set shortly after midnight. This situation would allow enough light for the paratroopers, yet ensure total darkness for the amphibious operations. The timing guaranteed that the last units to drop would have only a matter of minutes to assemble prior to moonset.[17] Any delay in the drop, or of the flights from departure airfields located in North Africa, meant dropping and assembling in total darkness.

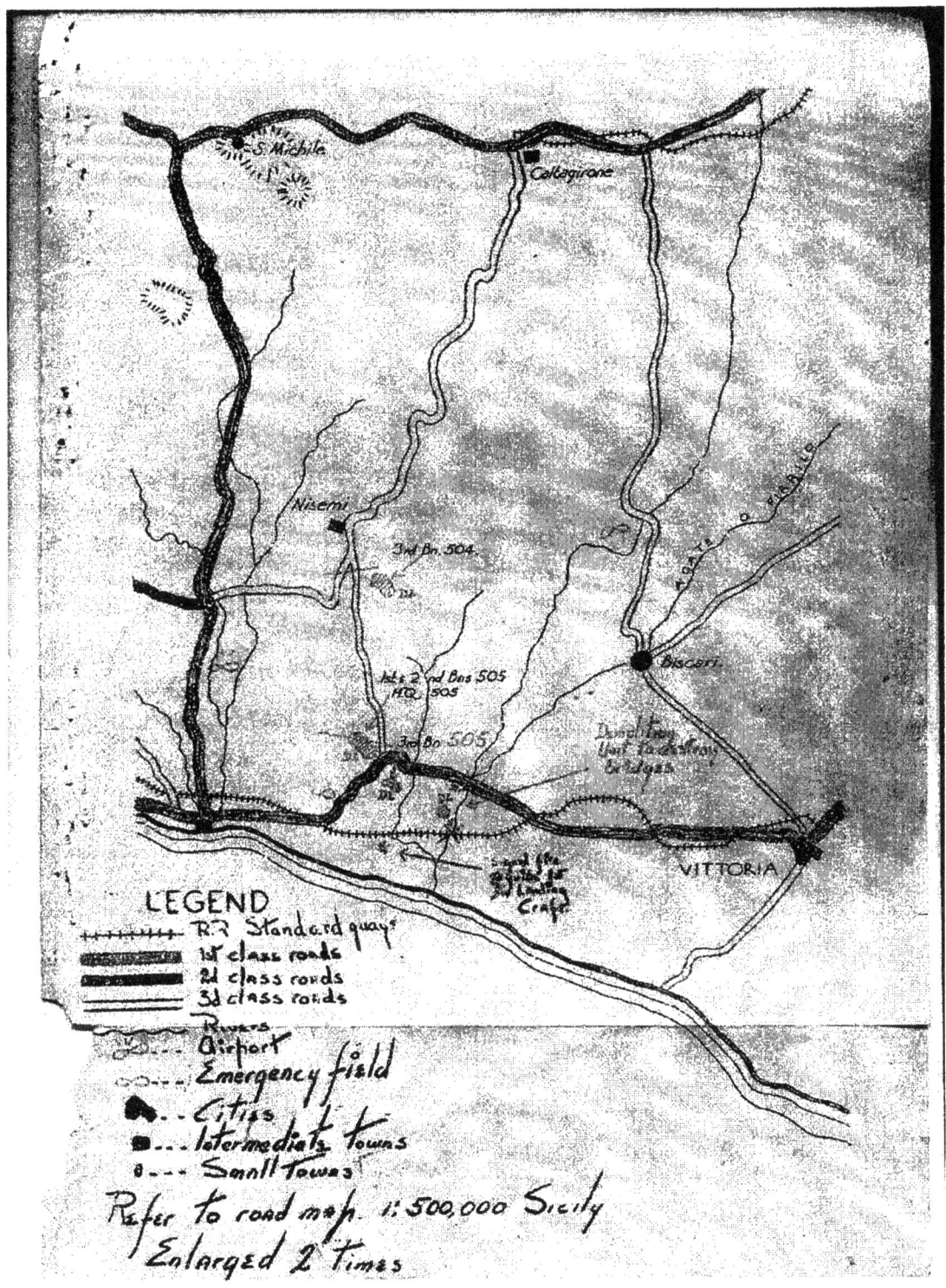

Figure 3. 505th RCT Planned DZs. Scanned from C. Billingslea, *Report of Airborne Operations, "Husky" and "Bigot"* (Headquarters, Fifth Army Airborne Training Center, 15 August 1943), figure 1.

During the planning phase of the operation, steps were taken to identify flight routes and establish aerial checkpoints one month prior to the operation, under the exact conditions, time and moon period, that would be present on the night of the assault.[18] In order to avoid the Allied naval fleet steaming towards Sicily, the flight route consisted of a direct eastward course from Tunisia to Malta. Aircraft would then veer north into the objective areas.[19] What normally would have been a 250-mile direct flight from the departure airfields to the drop zones had become a 420-mile twisting and turning course.[20]

A few major problems between the 82nd Airborne and its supporting air component, the 52nd Troop Carrier Command (TCC), would prove detrimental to operations. First, no unity of command existed between the Army Air Corps and 82nd Airborne Division. The 52nd TCC attached an Air Corps Liaison Officer to the 82nd, but he did not operate as an integral member of the Division staff and was not in a position to coordinate aircraft requirements. Second, and perhaps most glaringly the flight crews were not trained for conducting night airborne operations. The lack of a unified command over the Airborne and Air units complicated combined training efforts. Two large airborne training drops were conducted during daylight hours, even though the actual operation was to be conducted at night. The 52nd TCC also put very little effort into checking the location of pinpoint DZs at night. Meanwhile, the final weeks leading up to the operation saw the 52nd engaged in shuttling troops and supplies to advance bases, thus eliminating opportunities for a full-scale rehearsal. Despite all the training shortcomings, a tremendous spirit of cooperation existed between the 82nd and the 52nd. Nonetheless, inadequate organization proved to be a stumbling block.[21]

The 505th RCT conducted its departure from airfields in North Africa flawlessly and began flying towards Sicily. As the sun set over the Mediterranean, a heavy wind rose, and formations drifted off course from their assigned DZs. The United States pilots preferred flying the *V of Vs*, in which nine aircraft would fly in formation. This technique allowed for the massing of paratroopers on the ground and required less navigational skill, but made maneuverability while under fire difficult.[22]

Many flying formations broke up as organization began to deteriorate. Many navigators had only a remote idea of their locations and had either old air charts or no charts at all. As aircraft drifted over the armada located on the seas below, nervous gunners began to engage the transports with every available gun, further disrupting flight formations. In the end, when the 505th PIR dropped, very few units actually landed on their assigned drop zones. In fact, some of the paratroopers were dropped as far as 60 miles from their objectives.[23]

Though American airborne troops were spread across such a wide area of Sicily, the initiative they displayed, often individually or in small groups, played a decisive role in the success of the larger operation. Finding themselves lost, outnumbered, and often leaderless, paratroopers began assembling in small groups and conducted operations. Paratroopers carried out demolitions, cut lines of communications, established inland roadblocks, ambushed German and Italian motorized columns, captured prisoners often in excess of their own strength, and caused confusion over such an extensive area behind the enemy lines, that initial Axis reports estimated the number of parachutists dropped to be over ten times the actual number participating.[24] Paratroopers destroyed pillboxes and attacked the Italian defenders from the rear to clear the way for the amphibious forces inland.

Indicative of the spirit displayed by the paratroopers, the battle at Biazza Ridge stands out as an example of overcoming tremendous odds in the face of the enemy.[25] COL Gavin led a "rag-tag" group, 82nd paratroopers and 45th Infantry Division soldiers, in blocking an attack by the Herman Goering Division against the exposed western flank of the 45th as it moved inland from the beaches.

Gavin's group of 250 soldiers consisted of engineers, cooks, orderlies, riggers, clerks, and riflemen from numerous units. They lacked field guns, antitank guns, tanks, and were vastly outnumbered. Facing German artillery, mortars, infantry, and 60 ton Tiger tanks, the motley group succeeded in stopping an Axis counterattack with naval gunfire, 155-mm artillery from the 45th Division, 2.36-inch bazookas, and small arms.[26] General Karl Student candidly remarked in 1945 that:

> The Allied airborne operations in Sicily were decisive despite widely scattered drops which must be expected in a night landing. It is my opinion that if it had not been for the Allied airborne forces blocking the Hermann Göring Division's tanks from reaching the beachhead, that division would have driven the initial sea-borne forces back into the sea. I attribute the entire success of the Allied Sicilian operation to the delaying of the German reserves until sufficient forces had been landed by sea to resist the counter-attacks by our defending forces (the strength of which had been held in mobile reserve).[27]

In perhaps one of the most appalling instances of fratricide during World War II, twenty-three C-47s, loaded with paratroopers from the 504th Parachute Infantry Regiment, were shot down by friendly naval and ground antiaircraft fire on 11 July while attempting the planned airborne reinforcement behind friendly lines. 318 paratroopers, including the Assistant Division Commander, Brigadier General Charles Keerans, and scores of transport aircrews were killed during the operation.[28] Friendly fire forced the 52nd TCC pilots to conduct evasive maneuvers, forcing them from planned air routes. Those paratroopers who were able to exit their aircraft experienced the same dispersion problems that the 505th had suffered forty-eight hours earlier (See Figure 4).

Though historians may debate the success or failure of the 82nd Airborne in Sicily, the operation constituted a successful application of airborne doctrine. The United States entered the Sicily campaign with doctrine still evolving over the use of airborne troops. FM 31-30 expanded upon the limited roles outlined in FM 100-5 by envisioning using parachute troops to create confusion and to act as a diversion to the operations of the main force. Airborne forces might seize and hold key terrain in the rear of organized beach defenses in conjunction with naval operations, attack defended positions in the rear or flank, consolidate and hold gains made until the arrival of other friendly forces,[29] all of which the paratroopers accomplished. LTC William T. Ryder, an observer from the Airborne Command who participated in the operation, remarked that:

> The prescribed missions were not carried out successfully, but the employment of parachute troops was MOST successful. The bulk of parachutists were scattered and not dropped in the proper sector, consequently any action as a forceful regimental combat team was never accomplished. However, the aggressive action taken up by ALL parachutists after landing was a decided factor in the successful landing and advance of the sea borne troops.[30]

Though the drops were scattered throughout the southeast of Sicily, paratroopers played a key role in attaining the overall operational objective of seizing a foothold on Sicily. Prisoners taken on Sicily estimated that between ten and twenty thousand paratroopers were dropped on D-1. In the area of Marina de Ragusa, enemy units withdrew about 10 miles from the landing beaches due to the presence of paratroopers in their rear.[31]

Resupply operations plagued the airborne force throughout the entire operation. To compensate for this shortcoming, paratroopers were trained in foreign weapons while in North Africa. The course did not go into depth, but rather focused on familiarization with Axis rifles, carbines, mortars, machine pistols, machine guns, and artillery up to the German 88mm.[32] This training proved critical as soldiers replaced lost weapons with captured weapons to augment existing systems or to compensate for friendly ammunition shortages

Operational experience in Sicily proved valuable despite all of the mistakes. The 82nd Airborne, as well as the Airborne Command, learned many lessons in Sicily which contributed to the success of future operations in the ETO.

Each parachute artillery battalion consisted of three batteries of four 75mm pack howitzers. Each 75mm had to be broken down into nine pieces and mounted beneath the aircraft in separate bundles. Ammunition would be stored in similar bundles and mounted either under the aircraft or tossed out through the fuselage door. Once on the ground, all howitzers and ammunition was muscled around the battlefield.[33] Because of scattered drops, artillery batteries had difficulty locating and assembling the 75mm howitzers. Work was slow and some guns were never recovered. Three were utilized in the action on Biazza Ridge and proved effective in an anti-tank role, as well as for providing indirect fire support. Other than demonstrating the need for transport of both

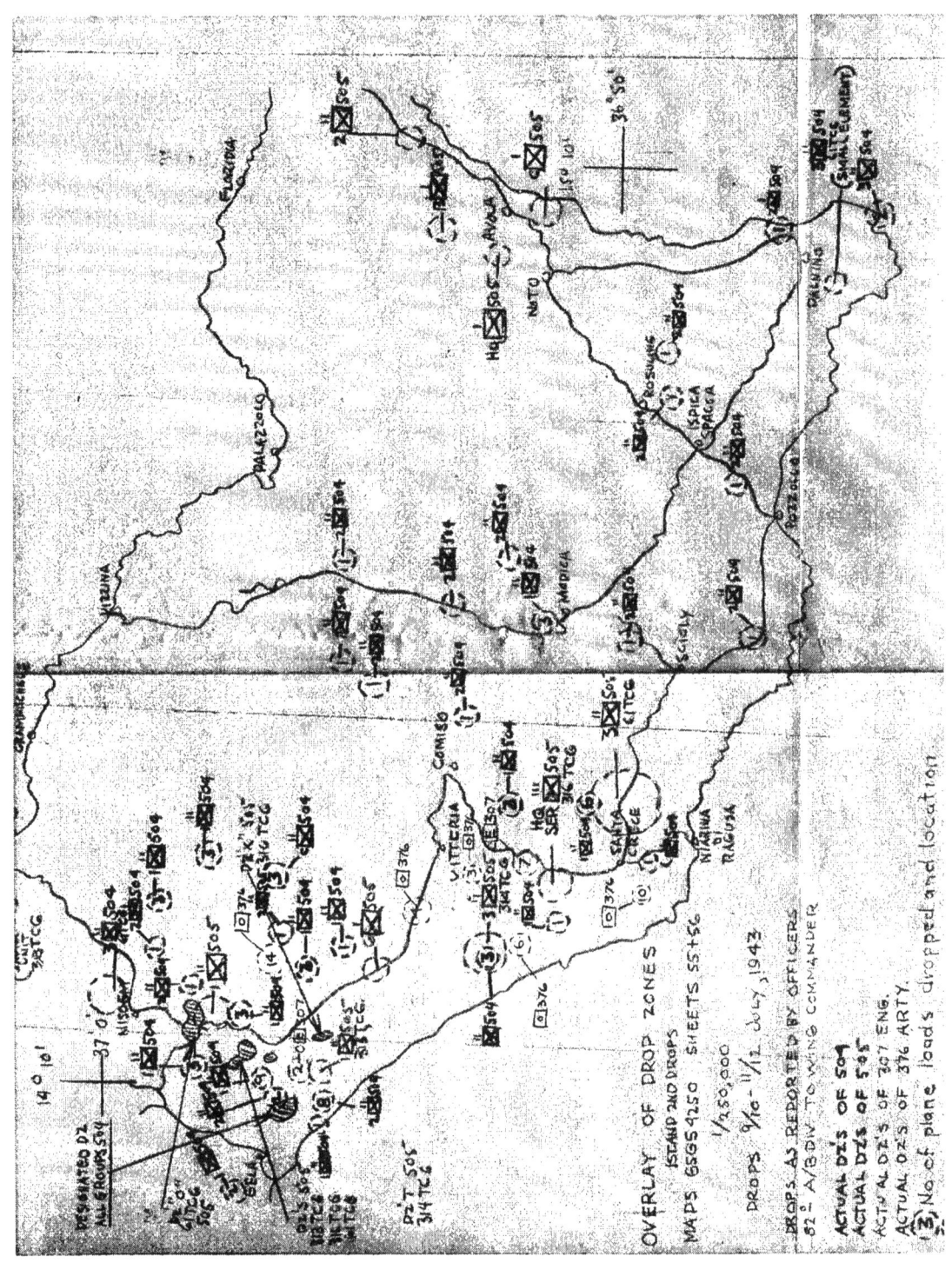

Figure 4. Actual Landings of 505th and 504th. Scanned from C. Billingslea, *Report of Airborne Operations, "Husky" and "Bigot"* (Headquarters, Fifth Army Airborne Training Center, 15 August 1943), figure 2.

the guns and ammunition on the ground, the operation did not provide a valid test for parachute artillery.[34]

The parachute artillery issue continued to plague the airborne community throughout the remainder of World War II, but the lessons of Sicily were well learned. The 101st Airborne dropped only one battalion of howitzers during the Normandy invasion, choosing to send the other two battalions "over the beach" to reduce the risk of losing significant numbers in the event of missed drops. Of the twelve howitzers dropped on D-Day, eleven were lost and not replaced until D+20. Of the twenty-four that came ashore, all were in action by D+2 in support of ground operations.[35]

To avoid the perils of dispersion over wide areas in the enemy rear, airborne planners took steps to improve delivery accuracy on assigned DZs. Pathfinder teams composed of experienced pilots and paratroopers were created to drop twenty minutes prior to an airborne assault. Composed of one officer and nine enlisted men, they would be equipped with electronic gear to serve as homing beacons. Additionally, the pathfinders would mark DZs with lights and assist in the assembly and reorganization of landing paratroopers.[36]

In an effort to eliminate the risk of fratricide, it was recommended that troops should never drop behind their own lines. Additionally, over water routes for transport aircraft should be ten miles wide and cleared of all shipping.

To a large segment of senior American military leaders, operations in Sicily seemed to demonstrate the cost and futility of large airborne operations. The Secretary of

War, Henry L. Stimson, tended to share this view, and LTG Lesley J. McNair, the Commanding General of the Army Ground Forces, proposed that the airborne divisions be broken up, with their parachute elements set up as non-divisional units, and their remaining elements organized as a light divisions and given broad general training.[37]

McNair later wrote:

> After the airborne operations in Africa and Sicily, my staff and I had become convinced of the impracticability of handling large airborne units. I was prepared to recommend to the War Department that airborne division be abandoned in our scheme of organization and that the airborne effort be restricted to parachute units of battalion size or smaller.[38]

General Eisenhower, writing from North Africa to General Marshall, also suggested a reorganization:

> I do not believe in the airborne division. I believe that airborne troops should be reorganized in self-contained units, comprising infantry, artillery, and special services, all of about the strength or a regimental combat team. Even if one had all the air transport he could possibly use the fact is at any given time and in any given spot only a reasonable number of air transports can be operated because of technical difficulties. To employ at any time and place a whole division would require a dropping over such an extended area that I seriously doubt that a division commander could regain control and operate the scattered forces as one unit. In any event, if these troops were organized in smaller, self-contained units, a senior commander, with a small staff and radio communications, could always be dropped in the area to insure necessary coordination.[39]

In contrast, General Ridgway believed that concentrated airborne operations were possible and that all the mistakes made in Sicily could be corrected. Major General Joseph Swing, the former Allied Forces Headquarters airborne advisor, protested that the views of McNair and Eisenhower were based upon a campaign marked by certain adverse conditions that were remediable. Swing pointed out that the Markham valley operation in New Guinea served as an example of what a properly trained airborne force could accomplish following exact planning and coordination with a major ground effort.[40]

In the end, a study conducted by the American and British Combined Staff Planners determined that nothing observed during combat operations, by either country, indicated that a division was not the proper organization for airborne troops. So, the hurdle was overcome. Had airborne forces lost the division structure and reversed back to battalion or regimental-sized units, they would have been no more effective than if they had retained the same mission originally contemplated for them in the early days of development. Where Crete was the graveyard for the German airborne forces, Sicily almost became the graveyard for American airborne forces.

Airborne proponents pleaded for a chance to demonstrate the capabilities of an airborne division. As plans were drawn up for the invasion of mainland Italy, they included the 82nd Airborne Division. A near perfect drop of the 504th and 505th PIRs in vicinity of Salerno, Italy proved that airborne warfare had evolved far beyond its embryonic origins. Actions in the Mediterranean Theater disproved many of the critics, but more importantly, spurred further growth in manpower, material, and expectations. All three were key components in the Cross-Channel invasion and in the roles that airborne forces would play in June 1944.

---

[1]Ridgway, 68-69.

[2]Devlin, 208.

[3]Lewis H. Brereton, *The Brereton Diaries* (New York, William Morrow and Company, 1946) 177.

[4] Devlin, 210.

[5] Brereton, 207.

[6] Warren, 22.

[7] Dwight D. Eisenhower, *Commander-in-Chief's Dispatch: Sicilian Campaign* (Allied Force Headquarters, 1943) 13.

[8] Tugwell, 158.

[9] James M. Gavin, *Airborne Assault Operations* (In Field, Sicily, Headquarters, 505th Parachute Infantry, 14 August 1943) 1-6. The 505th RCT consisted of the HQ, 505th PIR, 1-505th PIR, 2-505th PIR, 3-505th PIR, 3-504th PIR, B/307th EN, and the 456th PFAB.

[10] C. Billingslea, *Report of Airborne Operations, "Husky" and "Bigot"* (Headquarters, Fifth Army Airborne Training Center, 15 August 1943) 7.

[11] Blair, 73. Patton had insisted upon both the 505th and 504th PIR dropping on D-1. Over 100 C-47s were dedicated to the British airborne effort on Sicily. Ridgway was almost relieved by Eisenhower's Chief of Staff, MG Bedell Smith for not "cooperating" with the British when raising objections to the lack of aircraft dedicated to the 82nd. Ridgway felt he was "fighting for the needs of my command" and where lives were in the balance, he would not allow his command to be penalized merely for the sake of Allied "harmony." Had it not been for the intervention of Patton on Ridgway's behalf, the WWII, Korean War, and diplomatic legacy of Matthew Ridgway might have ended before it ever started.

[12] C. Billingslea, *Report of Airborne Operations, "Husky" and "Bigot,"* 8.

[13] Ibid.

[14] Ibid.

[15] Ibid.

[16] Ibid.

[17] Eisenhower, 20-21. In Eisenhower's dispatch, he cited the timing of the operation as being a "practical compromise between the 'irreconcilable' demands of the Navy for darkness and of the airborne forces for light."

[18] James M. Gavin, *Airborne Warfare* (Washington, D.C., Infantry Journal Press, 1947) 5.

[19] Devlin, 213.

[20] William B. Breuer, *Drop Zone Sicily* (Novato, CA, Presidio Press, 1983) 29.

[21] C. Billingslea, 3-4.

[22] Tugwell, 163-164.

[23] Hickey, 101-102.

[24] T.B. Ketterson, *82nd Airborne Division in Sicily and Italy, 9 July 1943, 13 September 1943, 22 January 1944* (Official Division Historical Records, no publisher) 38.

[25] It is interesting to note that the 505th had imbedded media with them on Biazza Ridge. John H. "Beaver" Thompson, a 34 year old correspondent from the Chicago Tribune, conducted his second combat parachute jump with the 505th at Sicily, his first being with the 509th in North Africa. One of the first jumpers he linked up with after the jump was none other than LTC Ryder. Much of what is written on Biazza Ridge was due to Thompson's reporting.

[26] Breuer, 143-157.

[27] Gavin, *Soldier*, 16.

[28] Breuer, 169.

[29] War Department. FM 31-30: *Tactics and Technique of Air-Borne Troops*. (Washington, D.C., US Government Printing Office, 20 May 1942) para. 41-42.

[30] William T. Ryder, *Report on American Airborne Phase of Operation Husky* (Headquarters Airborne Command, Army Ground Forces, 1943) 35. LTC Ryder participated in Operation Husky as an observer, and his presence has been speculated that in addition to recording the events for the Airborne Command, he was also available to assume command of a battalion based on projected leadership casualties. He is most renowned as serving as the Platoon Leader for the Airborne Test Platoon in 1940.

[31] Billingslea, 12.

[32] Ibid., 14.

[33] Blair, 41.

[34] Billingslea, 11.

[35] C. B. Anderson, *Employment of 75mm Pack Howitzers Dropped by Parachute in Airborne Divisions* (War Department Observer Board, HQ, Communications Zone, ETO, 1 August 1944) 1.

[36] Gavin, *On to Berlin,* 49-50.

[37] Greenfield, Palmer and Wiley, 346.

[38] Warren, 54.

[39] General Eisenhower letter to General Marshall, as quoted in Garland, Symthe, and Blumenson, 425.

[40] Garland, Symthe, and Blumenson, 425. In September 1943, the 503rd Parachute Infantry Regiment conducted an airborne assault in vicinity of Nazdeb, New Guinea along the Markham River. The paratroopers cut off Japanese troops as they attempted to withdraw from Lae and Salamauam, and seized an airfield upon which the entire Australian 7th Division airlanded. The mission in and of itself served as another success for the SWPA forces during Operation Cartwheel. The first airborne operation of the war in the Pacific Theater was executed with near perfection and very light casualties.

CHAPTER 6

CONCLUSION

The invasion and subsequent occupation of Crete had not been, and would not prove, essential to German strategy. A successful attempt on a more important objective, such as the islands of Malta or Cyprus, would by contrast have justified any loss suffered by its mounting. The impact of losing those two islands would have upset the British balance of power in the Mediterranean more than Crete. Hitler's disappointment with the operation was apparent. He refused to allow the German propaganda machine to publicize the operation while it was in progress. Viewing Crete as the "graveyard" of German parachute operations, he opposed future airborne operations of the same type.

The United States drew a conclusion different from Hitler's. In the eyes of American military planners, it was the particular form, rather than the underlying principle of airborne operations, which had proved unsound.[1] The Germans attempted to operate beyond its own means and tried to do too much at Crete.

In Sicily, the Allied airborne forces were risked in a large-scale airborne offensive in coordination with a major amphibious assault from the sea. Used in this manner, the 82nd Airborne Division distracted the Axis forces from concentrating against the amphibious assault. The presence of sea-borne troops likewise prevented the defenders from a concerted response against the fragile military instruments of the glider and parachute. The chief difference between Crete and Sicily lay in the application of airborne forces as part of a combined arms operation. The Germans attempted to use their airborne forces in a more independent manner. Their sea-borne and air-land forces only supported the parachute and glider forces. The United States reversed the terms of this strategy; in more modern terms, the 82nd Airborne Division served as a supporting operation in the campaign, while the amphibious forces were the decisive operation.

Still, in some respects airborne operations in Sicily shared similarities to the German airborne operation in Crete. In each case the attacker considered the operation a disappointment, while the defenders considered the operation more or less a spectacular success. Each operation was something of a turning point in the airborne effort of each side. For the Germans, Crete was the end of major airborne operations. For the United States, Sicily served as the beginning of airborne operations on an even larger scale.

The German use of airborne forces during World War II demonstrated the utility of specialized troops, used in a manner and on a scale only dreamed of previously, and served as impetus for expansion of the United States Army's own program. The airborne warfare model developed by the United States was neither a replica of the German model nor an entirely original product. The model the United States Army developed was something of a hybrid concept based upon the experiences and lessons of both countries.

Before May 1941, the United States had given no thought to developing an airborne organization larger than a battalion, as the initial doctrine reflected. The German experience in Crete showed what a large combined arms organization could achieve utilizing airborne techniques. This perception spurred rapid expansion within the United States in areas of doctrine and organization, further fueled by entry into the war in late 1941.

Historians often discuss the relationship among history, theory, and doctrine. History provides both the evidence and laboratory for theory. Often on the basis of combat experience, military theorists develop new ideas and methods of waging warfare. The amalgam translates into doctrine based upon a nation's accepted theory, capabilities, and priorities. During times of peace, the process can take years to develop, since many extraneous factors enter the calculus. As so often occurs during times of war, a nation may be forced to work through the process on a significantly compressed timeline. As the preeminent scholar Michael Howard stated, "Usually everybody starts even and everybody starts wrong…the advantage goes to the side which can most *quickly* adjust itself to the new and unfamiliar environment and learn from its mistakes."[2]

In 1941, the United States had it wrong in the field of airborne warfare. Doctrine, organization, material, and tactics lacked emphasis, originality, and inspiration within the small airborne community, and also in the Army as a whole. The Germans too had it wrong. They tried to do too much at Crete and, though operationally successful, they paid a heavy price and never attempted a large-scale airborne operation throughout the remainder of the war.

However, German operations served as a catalyst for the United States. Using Crete as the historical model of possibilities, airborne planners within the Army began to develop ideas and theories, going beyond the small-scale expectations that dominated the pages of FM 100-5. This development created a domino effect within the War Department, since doctrine and organizational changes created significant second and third order effects. The new capabilities that an expanded airborne force would bring to waging warfare were considerable, and they created technological challenges. Between May 1941 and the invasion of Sicily in July 1943, the United States airborne got the technological dimension right for the most part, but suffered numerous setbacks in application of the new doctrine. Airborne forces successfully accomplished their missions in Sicily, though not as planned (missed drop zones). Equipment proved effective when it could be brought to bear (75 mm artillery), and the C-47 proved to be a reliable aircraft, only the proficiency of the aircrews and fratricide hindered the concentrated assembly of the paratroopers on the ground. The difference between the United States and Germany though existed in the level of commitment. Armed with new historical precedent, the American airborne community recorded the lessons learned, adjusted, and continued to practice large-scale airborne assaults throughout the remainder of the war.

Many of the lessons learned with respect to history, theory, and doctrine during this expansion period of the U.S. Army's airborne capabilities remain appropriate to the development of the Objective Force in the 21st Century. Currently, the Objective Force is entirely doctrine and capabilities based. Organization, equipment, and force structure designs continue to evolve along with developments in science and technology, just as was the case with airborne forces in the early 1940s.

Those who do not study history are probably doomed to repeat it. Michael Howard described a view held by many professional soldiers during World War II. If the Army fails to transform properly, Howard's observation just may be applicable to the U.S. Army of the 21st Century.

> They [airborne forces] were believed to divert useful manpower to activities that were intermittent, usually marginal and invariably over publicized. Their wartime

operations were often seen as luxuries sustained by the patient and unspectacular efforts of their more self-effacing colleagues, and their activities did not appear to make much contribution to the massive and collective destruction of which war now inevitably consisted.[3]

Russian folk wisdom perhaps captures Howard's wisdom more succinctly in a proverb that asserts, "a wise person learns from other people's mistakes, while a fool learns from his own."

BIBLIOGRAPHICAL ESSAY

The information pertinent this thesis is derived from several types of principle sources: official government archival papers, Department of Defense publications and studies, published histories, memoirs and first hand accounts.

Of the archival papers, the most valuable were those of the 82nd Airborne Division during the Sicily and Italy campaigns located in the Combined Arms Research Library (CARL) at Fort Leavenworth, Kansas. The accounts of the Division Historian, LTC T.B. Ketterson, are well organized and extensive. They include background on the organization of the division, combat reports of the 504th and 505th PIRs, and numerous facts and statistics during actions in both Sicily and Italy.

Included in CARL's archives are various reports from Headquarters Airborne Command, Army Ground Forces. Of particular interest is LTC William Ryder's accurate and credible report on the American Airborne Phase of Operation Husky. LTC Ryder served as the platoon leader of the Airborne Test Platoon and is considered an airborne pioneer, who continued to develop doctrine from the start of the U.S. Army's airborne effort and throughout all European Theater operations.

The account by the United States Military Attaché to Egypt, Major Bonner Fellers, is found on microfilm in CARL and provided a colorful description of the German invasion of Crete. The Fellers account contained numerous observations, conclusions, and recommendations to the War Department that the U.S. Army adopted. Many of the airborne pioneers read his account and credited him with spurring efforts towards expansion.

Of the Department of Defense (DOD) publications, many proved invaluable. For insights into German parachute operations by former officers of the Wehrmacht, *Airborne Operations: A German Appraisal*; *The German Campaigns in the Balkans*; and *World War II German Military Studies, volume 13, The Mediterranean Theater*; and *Enemy Air-Borne* (sic) *Forces* are indispensable for a researcher looking to draw comparisons between the United States and German developments. CARL's archives also contain numerous Wehrmacht reports that could prove valuable to any researcher fluent in German.

While researching the doctrinal foundations and developments for both the United States and Germany, several manuals and reports formed the basis for research. Field Manual 100-5, *Operations*, dated 22 May 1941, and Field Manual 31-30, *Tactics and Technique of Air-Borne* (sic) *Troops*, dated 20 May 1942, portrayed the prescribed uses of American airborne forces before and after the German invasion of Crete. The evolution of doctrine is apparent in a comparison of the two manuals and enlightened my conclusions. Christopher R. Gabel's *The U.S. Army GHQ Maneuvers of 1941*, though covering a wide array of emerging doctrine, organization, and equipment throughout the

U.S. Army, provided excellent insight on initial perceptions among senior field leaders of how airborne forces might be utilized. Edward Luttwak's historical analysis, *The German Army of the Second World War, The Parachute Troops: the Fallschirmjaeger Formations*, combined with DOD publications written by former German officers, provided important data on German doctrine, organizational developments, tactics, and operations throughout the entire war.

Numerous first hand accounts and memoirs cover all areas of World War II. Those of interest to any historian researching airborne operations are General James M Gavin's works *On to Berlin* and *Airborne Warfare*. Though both proved invaluable, *On to Berlin* provided the best insight covering all facets of my research and incorporating most of his previously published works. General Matthew B. Ridgway's *Soldier* was interesting, but lacked depth in World War II and airborne development because of a larger focus on his entire remarkable service career. Martin Pöppel's *Heaven & Hell: The War Diary of a German Paratrooper* provided not only a personal account of operations in Crete, but also all other operations throughout his entire service during World War II. General Louis H. Brereton's *The Brereton Diaries* failed to provide any valuable insights, partly due to his late engagement with the airborne effort.

Though not of significant research value, but nevertheless fascinating and deeply moving, Ross Carter's *Those Devil's in Baggy Pants* provided another perspective on airborne warfare. Written from the enlisted man's point of view, the book provided a squad and platoon level view of airborne training and operations in the 504th PIR.

Of the 82nd Airborne Division's official histories, the *Saga of the All American*, edited by Forrest W. Dawson, is disappointing. A mere picture book and overview of divisional history, it is error-prone and poorly written.

The United States Air Force Historical study, *Airborne Missions in the Mediterranean, 1942-1945,* by John C. Warren, is outstanding. Part one of a two-volume monograph this work provided very useful information on parallel developments within airborne warfare and transport aircraft materially, doctrinally, and operationally. Less noteworthy and heavily canted with regard to airborne operations is the official *Army Air Forces in World War II*, by Wesley F. Craven and James L. Cate.

Of the many works produced by professional writers and historians covering World War II, few covered airborne operations exclusively. Of the works that covered efforts in airborne warfare by numerous countries, Michael Hickey's *Out of the Sky,* John R. Galvin's *Air Assault: The Development of Airmobile Warfare,* and Maurice Tugwell's *Airborne to Battle* are by far the preeminent works. Gerard M. Devlin's *Paratrooper: The Saga of U.S. Army and Marine Parachute and Glider Combat Troops During World War II*, an extremely thorough work, provided the best insight into American airborne warfare developments.

For the German perspective, James Lucas' work *Storming Eagles: German Airborne Forces in World War II*, proved both accurate and moving. Lucas affords an interesting perspective, having fought against and been captured by German parachutists as a British infantryman in World War II.

In an effort to compare both American and German airborne forces, I focused on two operations: Crete in 1941 and Sicily in 1943. Alan Clark's *The Fall of Crete* and William B. Breuer's *Drop Zone Sicily* far surpassed any other works that I encountered in my research that specifically addressed the two actions. Well written and poignant, both were factually accurate, captivating, and dramatic. Somewhat biased towards the British and American sides, neither allowed these biases to interfere with their relevancies.

Finally, Clay Blair's *Ridgway's Paratroopers: The American Airborne in World War II* was the work that initiated my interest in the topic of the development of U.S. Army airborne warfare was. Part biography, part historical work, Blair effectively traced airborne developments and actions of all airborne units participating in the European Theater of Operations. Initially heavily focused on the 82nd Airborne Division, it never seemed to portray any bias, while chronologically tracing developments and operations with balanced exposure. It remains the most relevant work to me as a historian, but more so to me personally and professionally as a five year veteran of the 82nd Airborne Division being reassigned to the 3rd Battalion, 504th Parachute Infantry Regiment.

---

[1] John Keegan, The Second World War (New York, Penguin Books, 1989) 172.

[2] Michael Howard, "Military Science in an Age of Peace," *RUSI, Journal of the Royal United Services Institute for Defense Studies* 119 (March 1974); reprinted in US Army Command and General Staff College, *C610 Syllabus/Book of Readings*, (Fort Leavenworth: USACGSC, August 1997), 27.

[3] Bellamy, 87.

APPENDIX A

U.S. AND GERMAN RANK EQUIVALENTS

U.S. Army and Army Air Forces	**German Army and *Luftwaffe***
General of the Army	Generalfeldmarschall
General	Generaloberst
Lieutenant General	General der Infantrie, Flieger, etc.
Major General	Generalleutnant
Brigadier General	Generalmajor
Colonel	Oberst
Lieutenant Colonel	Oberstleutnant
Major	Major
Captain	Hauptmann or Rittmeister
1st Lieutenant	Oberleutnant
2nd Lieutenant	Leutnant
First Sergeant	Stabsfeldwebel
Sergeant	Feldwebel
Corporal	Unteroffizier
Private	Schutze

Source: Maurice Tugwell, *Airborne To Battle: A History of Airborne Warfare 1918-1971.* (London: William Kimber and Co., 1971), 354.

GLOSSARY

Airborne units. Combat organizations that arrive on the battlefield during forced entry operations. Units may be comprised of air-land, glider, parachute or any combination of the three.

Air-land forces. Combat units that are designated to fly on powered aircraft and land on prepared or improvised airfields, normally following forced entry operations by parachute or glider forces.

Fallschirmjaeger. A German paratrooper.

Glider forces. Combat units that are designated to fly in gliders during forced entry operations and are normally assigned only to airborne units.

Parachute forces. Combat units that are designated to fly in powered aircraft and utilize parachutes to arrive on the battlefield during forced entry operations.

SOURCES CONSULTED

Primary Sources

Armed Forces Staff College Presentation. *Airborne Operations (Historical Presentation)*. Norfolk, VA: CARL Archives, Ft. Leavenworth, KS, N-15878.9, 1953.

Baldwin, Hanson W. "Skytroops." *New York Times* (26 October 1941): section M, page 4-5, 24-26.

Billingslea, C. HQ, Fifth Army Airborne Training Center, Memorandum to Chief of Staff, War Department, Subject: *Report of Airborne Operations "Huskey"* (sic) *and "Bigot"*. CARL Archives, Ft. Leavenworth, KS, N-6414, 15 August 1943.

_____. HQ Airborne Command, Army Ground Forces, Information Bulletin No. 2, Fort Bragg, NC, CARL Archives, Ft. Leavenworth, KS, N-3082, 24 November 1942.

Brereton, Lewis H. *The Brereton Diaries*. New York: William Morrow and Company, 1946.

Carter, Ross S. *Those Devils in Baggy Pants*. Kingsport, Tennessee: The Kingsport Press, 1951.

Chief of Military History, SSUSA. *The Airborne Team, 1941-1945*. No publisher, CARL Archives, Ft. Leavenworth, KS, N-17064, 1950.

Dawson, W. Forrest. *Saga of the All American*. Atlanta: Albert Love Enterprises, 1946.

Department of the Air Force. *Army Air Forces Statistical Digest*. Washington, D.C.: Director, Statistical Services, Comptroller, Headquarters, U.S. Air Force, June 1947.

Deichmann, Paul. *German Air Force Operations in Support of the Army*. Maxwell AFB, AL, USAF Historical Division, Research Studies Institute, 1962.

Department of the Army Pamphlet No. 20-232. *Airborne Operations: A German Appraisal*. Washington, D.C., CARL Archives, Ft. Leavenworth, KS, 20-232, 1951.

Department of the Army Pamphlet No. 20-260. *The German Campaign in the Balkans (Spring 1941)*. Washington, D.C., CARL Archives, Ft. Leavenworth, KS, 1953.

Detwiler, Donald S., ed. *World War II German Military Studies, Vol. 13*. New York: Garland Publishing, Inc., 1979.

Eisenhower, Dwight D. *Commander-in-Chiefs Dispatch – Sicilian Campaign*. Allied Force Headquarters, CARL Archives, Ft. Leavenworth, KS, R-13457, 1943.

Fellers, Bonner F. Military Intelligence Division, War Department General Staff, Military Attaché Report: Egypt, Subject: Air-Borne Invasion of Crete, CARL Archives, Ft. Leavenworth, KS, N-5842, 9 August 1941.

Gavin, James M. *Airborne Warfare*. Washington, D.C.: Infantry Journal Press, 1947.

_____. *On to Berlin*. New York: The Viking Press, 1978.

_____. HQ, 505th PIR, Memorandum to Commanding General, 82nd Airborne Division, Subject: Airborne Assault Operations, CARL Archives, Ft. Leavenworth, KS, N-12706, 14 August 1943.

_____. Report of the 505th Parachute Combat Team in the Landing on Sicily, CARL Archives, Ft. Leavenworth, KS, N-12705, In Field, No date.

_____. HQ 505th Combat Team, Memorandum to Commanding General, 82nd Airborne Division, Subject: Airborne Assault Operations, CARL Archives, Ft. Leavenworth, KS, N-12707, 22 October 1943.

Ketterson, T.B. *82nd Airborne Division in Sicily and Italy: 9 July 1943, 13 Sep 1943, 22 Jan 1944*. 82nd Airborne Division Official History, No publisher, CARL Archives, Ft. Leavenworth, KS, R-11960, 1943-1945.

Military Intelligence Division. *Battle of Crete: May 20 – June 1, 1941*. Washington, D.C., War Department, CARL Archives, Ft. Leavenworth, KS, R-16292, October 1941.

Military Intelligence Service. *Enemy Air-Borne Forces*. Washington, D.C.: War Department, CARL Archives, Ft. Leavenworth, KS, R-14161, 1942.

_____. *Notes and Lessons on Operations in the Middle East*. Washington, D.C.: War Department, CARL Archives, Ft. Leavenworth, KS, R-14355-2, 1943.

Patton, George S., Jr. HQ 7th Army, Notes on the Sicilian Campaign, CARL Archives, Ft. Leavenworth, KS, October 1943.

Pöppel, Martin. *Heaven & Hell: The War Diary of a German Paratrooper*. Kent, Great Britain: Spellmount Limited, 1988.

Porter, R.W., Jr. G-2 Periodic Report No. 5, HQ, 1st Infantry Division, CARL Archives, Ft. Leavenworth, KS, N-6414, 15 July 1943.

Ridgway, Matthew B. *Soldier: The Memoirs of Matthew B. Ridgway.* New York: Harper & Brothers, 1956.

Ringel, Julius. *Capture of Crete (May 1941).* Headquarters United States Army, Europe, Foreign Military Studies Branch, CARL Archives, Ft. Leavenworth, KS, N-5842.2-B, 1945.

Ryder, William. HQ Airborne Command, Army Ground Forces, Observer's Report on American Airborne Phase of Operation "Husky." CARL Archives, Ft. Leavenworth, KS, N-6443-2, 14 August 1943.

Tucker, Reuben. HQ, 504th PIR, Memorandum to Commanding General, 82nd Airborne Division, Subject: Airborne Assault Operations – 9-14 July 1943, CARL Archives, Ft. Leavenworth, KS, N-12704, 21 August 1943.

United States Army White Paper. "Concepts for the Objective Force." 2002.

United States Army White Paper. "Objective Force in 2015." 8 December 2002.

War Department. FM 100-5, *Operations.* Washington, D.C., US Government Printing Office, 22 May 1941.

War Department. FM 31-30: *Tactics and Technique of Air-Borne Troops.* Washington, D.C., US Government Printing Office, CARL Archives, Ft. Leavenworth, KS, 20 May 1942.

Warren, C.F. (LTC). Special Intelligence Report No. 69, *Lessons Learned from Recent Airborne Operations in Western Europe.* CARL Archives, Ft. Leavenworth, KS, N-6663, February 1945.

Warren, John C. *Airborne Missions in the Mediterranean: 1942-1945.* Maxwell AFB, AL: USAF Historical Studies: No. 74, USAF Historical Division, Air University, CARL Archives, Ft. Leavenworth, KS, N-16372.32, September 1955.

<u>Secondary Sources</u>

Autry, Jerry. *General William C. Lee: Father of the Airborne.* Raleigh, NC: Airborne Press, 1995.

Bellamy, Christopher. *The Evolution of Modern Land Warfare*. New York: Routledge, Chapman, & Hall Inc., 1990.

Blair, Clay. *Ridgway's Paratroopers: The American Airborne in World War II*. New York: Doubleday and Company, Inc., 1985.

Blumenson, Martin, B.F. Cooling, III, Ernest F. Fisher, Walter Hermes, Charles V. P. von Luttichau, Charles B. MacDonald, Billy C. Mossman, H. M. Wolfe. *Airborne Operations*. Washington, D.C., US Army Center of Military History, 1965.

Boston, Ronald G. "Doctrine by Default." *Air & Space Power Chronicles* (May/June 1983).

Breuer, William B. *Drop Zone Sicily*. Novato, California: Presidio Press, 1983.

Brucer, Marshall, ed. A History of Airborne Command and Airborne Center. Sharpsburg, MD: Antietam National Museum, 1979 reprint of 1946 edition.

Clark, Alan. *The Fall of Crete*. London: Cassell & Co., 1962.

Cox, Kenneth J. *The Battle for Crete (Operation Mercury): An Operational Analysis*. Newport, RI: Naval War College, 2001.

Devlin, Gerard M. *Paratrooper! The Saga of United States Army and Marine Parachute and Glider Combat Troops during World War II*. New York: St. Martin's Press, 1979.

Dupuy, Trevor N. *The Air War in the West: September 1939 – May 1941*. New York: Franklin Watts, Inc., 1963.

Gabel, Christopher R. *The U.S. Army GHQ Army Maneuvers of 1941*. Washington, D.C., Center of Military History, United States Army, 1991.

Galvin, John R. *Air Assault: The Development of Airmobile Warfare*. New York: Hawthorn Books, Inc., 1969.

Garland, Albert N., Howard M. Smyth, and Martin Blumenson. *United States Army in World War II - The Mediterranean Theater of Operations: Sicily and the Surrender of Italy*. Washington, D.C.: Center of Military History, United States Army, 1986.

Glantz, David M. *The Soviet Airborne Experience*. Ft. Leavenworth: Research Survey 5/Combat Studies Institute, United States Army Command and General Staff College, 1984.

Glines, Carroll V. *The Compact History of the United States Air Force*. New York: Hawthorn Books, Inc., 1963.

Greenfield, Kent R., Robert R. Palmer, and Bell I. Wiley. *United States Army in World War II - The Army Ground Forces: The Organization of Ground Combat Troops*. Washington, D.C.: Historical Division, Department of the Army, 1947.

Halberstadt, Hans. *Airborne: Assault from the Sky*. Novato, CA: Presidio Press, 1988.

Hickey, Michael. *Out of the Sky: A History of Airborne Warfare*. New York: Charles Scribner's Sons, 1979.

Holley, Irving B. Jr. *United States Army in World War II - Special Studies. Buying Aircraft: Materiel Procurement for the Army Air Forces*. Washington, D.C.: Office of the Chief of Military History, Department of the Army, 1964.

Howard, Michael. "Military Science in an Age of Peace," *RUSI, Journal of the Royal United Services Institute for Defense Studies* 119 (March 1974); reprinted in US Army Command and General Staff College, *C610 Syllabus/Book of Readings*, Fort Leavenworth: USACGSC, August 1997.

Keegan, John. *The Second World War*. New York: Penguin Books, 1989.

Larson, George A. "The Glider in World War II: The Waco CG-4A Combat Glider." *American Aviation Historical Society Journal*. (Volume 46 No. 4, Winter, 2001) Pages 270-279.

Lucas, James. *Storming Eagles: German Airborne Forces in World War Two*. London: Arms and Armour Press, 1988.

Luttwak, Edward N. *The German Army of the Second World War - The Parachute Troops: the Fallschirmjaeger Formations*. Ft. Monroe, VA, 1983.

Matloff, Maurice. "The American Approach to War, 1919-1945", *The Theory and Practice of War*, edited by Michael Howard (Bloomington, IN: Indiana University Press, 1975) 215-218.

Miksche, F.O. *Paratroops*. New York: Random House, 1943.

Smith, Carl, Mike Chappell. *US Paratrooper, 1941-45*. Oxford: Osprey Publishing, 2000.

Tugwell, Maurice. *Airborne To Battle: A History of Airborne Warfare 1918-1971*. London: William Kimber and Co., 1971.

INITIAL DISTRIBUTION LIST

Combined Arms Research Library
U.S. Army Command and General Staff College
250 Gibbon Ave.
Fort Leavenworth, KS 66027-2314

Defense Technical Information Center/OCA
825 John J. Kingman Rd., Suite 944
Fort Belvoir, VA 22060-6218

Dr. Bruce W. Menning
DJMO
USACGSC
1 Reynolds Ave.
Fort Leavenworth, KS 66027-1352

LTC Paul L. Cal
CSI
USACGSC
1 Reynolds Ave.
Fort Leavenworth, KS 66027-1352

LTC John A. Suprin
Department
USACGSC
1 Reynolds Ave.
Fort Leavenworth, KS 66027-1352

CERTIFICATION FOR MMAS DISTRIBUTION STATEMENT

1. Certification Date: 6 June 2003

2. Thesis Author: MAJ Thomas J. Sheehan

3. Thesis Title: World War II Vertical Envelopment: The German Influence on U.S. Army Airborne Operations

4. Thesis Committee Members:
   Signatures: _____
   _____
   _____

5. Distribution Statement: See distribution statements A-X on reverse, then circle appropriate distribution statement letter code below:

(A) B C D E F X   SEE EXPLANATION OF CODES ON REVERSE

If your thesis does not fit into any of the above categories or is classified, you must coordinate with the classified section at CARL.

6. Justification: Justification is required for any distribution other than described in Distribution Statement A. All or part of a thesis may justify distribution limitation. See limitation justification statements 1-10 on reverse, then list, below, the statement(s) that applies (apply) to your thesis and corresponding chapters/sections and pages. Follow sample format shown below:

EXAMPLE

Limitation Justification Statement	/	Chapter/Section	/	Page(s)
Direct Military Support (10)	/	Chapter 3	/	12
Critical Technology (3)	/	Section 4	/	31
Administrative Operational Use (7)	/	Chapter 2	/	13-32

Fill in limitation justification for your thesis below:

Limitation Justification Statement	/	Chapter/Section	/	Page(s)
_____	/	_____	/	_____
_____	/	_____	/	_____
_____	/	_____	/	_____
_____	/	_____	/	_____
_____	/	_____	/	_____

7. MMAS Thesis Author's Signature: _____

STATEMENT A: Approved for public release; distribution is unlimited. (Documents with this statement may be made available or sold to the general public and foreign nationals).

STATEMENT B: Distribution authorized to U.S. Government agencies only (insert reason and date ON REVERSE OF THIS FORM). Currently used reasons for imposing this statement include the following:

1. Foreign Government Information. Protection of foreign information.

2. Proprietary Information. Protection of proprietary information not owned by the U.S. Government.

3. Critical Technology. Protection and control of critical technology including technical data with potential military application.

4. Test and Evaluation. Protection of test and evaluation of commercial production or military hardware.

5. Contractor Performance Evaluation. Protection of information involving contractor performance evaluation.

6. Premature Dissemination. Protection of information involving systems or hardware from premature dissemination.

7. Administrative/Operational Use. Protection of information restricted to official use or for administrative or operational purposes.

8. Software Documentation. Protection of software documentation - release only in accordance with the provisions of DoD Instruction 7930.2.

9. Specific Authority. Protection of information required by a specific authority.

10. Direct Military Support. To protect export-controlled technical data of such military significance that release for purposes other than direct support of DoD-approved activities may jeopardize a U.S. military advantage.

STATEMENT C: Distribution authorized to U.S. Government agencies and their contractors: (REASON AND DATE). Currently most used reasons are 1, 3, 7, 8, and 9 above.

STATEMENT D: Distribution authorized to DoD and U.S. DoD contractors only; (REASON AND DATE). Currently most reasons are 1, 3, 7, 8, and 9 above.

STATEMENT E: Distribution authorized to DoD only; (REASON AND DATE). Currently most used reasons are 1, 2, 3, 4, 5, 6, 7, 8, 9, and 10.

STATEMENT F: Further dissemination only as directed by (controlling DoD office and date), or higher DoD authority. Used when the DoD originator determines that information is subject to special dissemination limitation specified by paragraph 4-505, DoD 5200.1-R.

STATEMENT X: Distribution authorized to U.S. Government agencies and private individuals of enterprises eligible to obtain export-controlled technical data in accordance with DoD Directive 5230.25; (date). Controlling DoD office is (insert).

www.ingramcontent.com/pod-product-compliance
Lightning Source LLC
Chambersburg PA
CBHW081258170426
43198CB00017B/2834